Arthy Muthanna Singh is a children's writer, freelance journalist, copywriter, editor and cartoonist. She has authored more than thirty-five books for children. She conducts creative writing workshops and has been helping her mother conduct the Ooty Literary Festival since 2016. Her present occupation is that of partner at SYLLABLES27, an outfit that produces books for children on a turn-key basis for publishers and organizations that work with children. Arthy lives in Gurugram and hopes to move to Goa someday.

Mamta Nainy is a children's writer and editor. She spent some years in advertising before an apple fell on her head while she was sitting under a mango tree, and she had her Eureka moment. She has been writing for children since. She has authored many books for children, including *A Brush with Indian Art,* which won the Hindu Young World-Goodbooks Awards 2019 in the Best Book Non-Fiction category, and *Bioscope*, a picture book that featured in the IBBY Honour List 2012.

A Dozen and a Half Stories

Strange and Mysterious Places the World Forgot

ARTHY MUTHANNA SINGH
MAMTA NAINY

Published by
Rupa Publications India Pvt. Ltd 2019
7/16, Ansari Road, Daryaganj
New Delhi 110002

Sales centres:
Allahabad Bengaluru Chennai
Hyderabad Jaipur Kathmandu
Kolkata Mumbai

Copyright © Arthy Muthanna Singh and Mamta Nainy 2019

Illustrations by Mistunee Chowdhury

The views and opinions expressed in this book are the authors' own and
the facts are as reported by them which have been verified to the extent
possible, and the publishers are not in any way liable for the same.
All rights reserved.

No part of this publication may be reproduced, transmitted,
or stored in a retrieval system, in any form or by any means,
electronic, mechanical, photocopying, recording or otherwise,
without the prior permission of the publisher.

ISBN: 978-93-5333-716-2

First impression 2019

10 9 8 7 6 5 4 3 2 1

The moral right of the authors has been asserted.

This book is sold subject to the condition that it shall not, by way
of trade or otherwise, be lent, resold, hired out, or otherwise circulated,
without the publisher's prior consent, in any form of binding
or cover other than that in which it is published.

To my mother, whose memory and grasp of history far outshine mine...
—*A.M.S.*

For Vedant, who can find mysteries even in the most mundane; and for Mum and Tito,
my great travelling partners.
—*M.N.*

Contents

Introduction ix

1. The Lake of Skeletons 1
2. A Monument with No Pillars 11
3. The Great Wall of India 21
4. A Tree or a Monument? 31
5. The Mini Taj 43
6. The Lake that Casts Moon Magic 55
7. The Hanging Pillar 67
8. The Honeycomb Monastery 75
9. A Relic of St. Philomena of Italy In India? 87
10. The Gate with a Bloody History 99
11. The Drowning Church 111
12. The Temple with Musical Pillars 117
12½. The Hide-and-Seek Beach 125

Acknowledgements 133

Introduction

'It happens only in India...'

Haven't we all heard this phrase ever so often? But have you ever wondered where this notion came from? Well, we've finally got an answer for you!

India is a wonderful country in more ways than you have ever imagined. Apart from being home to many colourful landscapes, big temples and ancient monuments that are popular tourist destinations, it also has strange and mysterious places that are off the beaten track. It truly has zillions of secrets buried deep in its most bizarre sites, which either leave people wide-eyed with shock or freak them out when they learn about them. Down neglected roads, beyond hidden doors and under the deep seas, these mysterious locales, bizarre sites and strange settings are shrouded by fascinating stories, unbelievable history and even a whole lot of spookiness!

In this book, we will take you on an armchair tour across the country to see some of these most oddly strange and mysterious places—places that seem straight out of a mystery novel—and let your imagination run wild! From an ancient lake of skeletons to a palace that has no pillars, from a gate that's believed to drip blood to a church that drowns in a reservoir and then mysteriously reappears, from a tree with no trunk to a one-of-a-kind crater created by a huge chip of the moon, these places will spook you, send shivers down your spine, make you gasp and leave you with more questions than answers!

Of course, you can't believe everything you hear! So the best approach to the information you'll encounter in these pages is to keep an open mind. Ferret out facts, ruminate on the rumours, analyse alternate explanations and come to your own conclusions. Who knows, maybe you'd be the one to unfold the secrets behind these mysterious places that many generations of scientists and historians have been puzzling, befuddling over!

So grab your mystery-busters' gear, strap yourself in and get ready for a truly unforgettable journey to the most mysterious places in India that you probably didn't even know existed!

1
The Lake of Skeletons
Roopkund Lake

The year was 1942. The sun was just waking up in the Himalayas—its rays nudging the snow-clad mountains and the rock-strewn glaciers to life. The Roopkund Lake was gurgling. A forest guard was hard at work as he navigated the steep and hilly terrain, picking his way through the valley. Just as he reached the edge of the lake, he saw something that sent shivers down his spine. He stood frozen, with his heart in his mouth. Hundreds of skulls and bones floated in the clear, turquoise waters of the Roopkund Lake, while some lay haphazardly on its shore—a striking contrast with the scenic beauty of the mountains. Something terrible must have happened here, but what? Who were these people? What were they doing in the inhospitable regions of the Himalayas? And how did their skeletons reach this lake that's tucked away in the desolate mountains?

A FROZEN GRAVEYARD

Ever since this discovery was made by the forest guard, the Roopkund Lake has been known by another name—the Skeleton Lake. In the brief summers that the Himalayas see between June and mid-October, the frozen lake melts—revealing its dark secrets. The remains have left anthropologists, scientists, historians and the local people scratching their heads for long; no one knows who these people were or where they came from! The initial assumption was that these remains belonged to the

Japanese soldiers who were trekking through the rough terrains of the Himalayas in a bid to invade India during World War II, and met a tragic fate. The British government, which was ruling India at that time, was terrified and sent a team of investigators to determine the truth. The remains of roughly 300 people were removed from the lake, some of whose flesh and hair had been partly preserved by the dry, cold air of the Himalayas. However, upon examination, they realized that these bones were not of Japanese soldiers, for they were quite old and not 'fresh enough'!

MYTHICAL BEGINNINGS

Roopkund Lake is a glacial lake, situated in the Himalayas, at an altitude of approximately 16,500 feet. Like many other Himalayan lakes, this one too has a mythological story attached to it. According to the myth, Lord Shiva and Goddess Parvati were on their way to Kailash. Goddess Parvati, before commencing on this journey, had killed demons. She wanted to have a bath but couldn't find any rivers or lakes nearby. Lord Shiva then dug his trishul (trident) into the mountain and created a lake. Goddess Parvati bathed in the pristine blue waters of this lake. The waters were so clear that she could easily see her reflection in it. From there came the name 'Roopkund'—'roop' meaning appearance and 'kund' meaning a small reservoir.

A CURSED KING OR A MASS SUICIDE?

Some scientists who studied the remains said that the bones date back to sometime between the 12th and the 15th centuries CE. Some believe that a group of people were trapped in the icy Himalayan slope and had no way to escape, and that's how they all died together. These lonely victims could have been pilgrims headed to the Nanda Devi mountain, revered as the abode of Nanda, the Hindu Goddess of Bliss. Also known as Raj Jat, or Royal Pilgrimage, this gruelling trek is undertaken by local villagers every twelve years, along a path that crosses Roopkund Lake.

A legend goes that, in the medieval times, King Jasidhwal of Kannauj and his pregnant wife were taking this pilgrimage to celebrate the impending birth of their child. However, Jasidhwal disregarded the rules of the pilgrimage by taking dancers and soldiers with him and by refusing to walk barefoot. His wife also gave birth to the child along the way, on the slope of the mountain. This earned him the wrath of Goddess Nanda who sent a great snowstorm and the lives of the king, the queen and their courtiers were cut short by the raging mountain goddess. Over time, landslides pushed their bodies into the otherwise pristine Roopkund Lake. Remains of jewellery and other artefacts are still found scattered among the skeletons, apart from many knives and spears, which only point at this theory more strongly. Also, among Himalayan women, there is a traditional folk song, whose lyrics suggest that once a goddess was so infuriated with outsiders who tarnished the sanctity of her mountain abode that she showed her anger by hurling hailstones at them, which were 'hard as iron'. These outsiders might have been the King of Kannauj and his troupe.

Some other theories propound that perhaps it was some sort of a ritual mass suicide. But why would so many people commit suicide together, and how? Well, no one knows for sure!

A NATURAL DISASTER

What was most intriguing about the skeletons found in the Roopkund Lake was that all of them bore strange blows on the skulls, as if hit by something the size of a cricket ball! But a concrete explanation to this had to wait for six decades after the forest guard found the skeletons in the lake. In 2004, an advanced scientific study was carried out, and the answer, eerily enough, was not too far from what the legend said. Some scientists studied the traces of round-shaped blows and cracks on the bones and found that the injuries to the skulls and shoulder bones of the skeletons were consistent with the victims being hit from above. These short, deep cracks didn't seem to be caused by a landslide or an avalanche but by blunt, round objects. The only plausible explanation for so many people sustaining such similar injuries at the same time is that perhaps something fell from the sky. Scientists believe that the deaths of these people were caused by extremely large hailstones. Presumably, they were 'iron-like' hailstones, just as the folklore says.

In addition to skeletons, the scientists also discovered some bodies with remnants of the flesh intact. They could find their hair and nails as well as pieces of clothing. They also found glass bangles, indicating the presence of women, and leather shoes and bamboo staves, which led them to hypothesize that the corpses were those of pilgrims. The scientists estimate that as many as 600 bodies may still be buried in snow and ice by the lake!

TWO IS BETTER THAN ONE

During the study conducted on these skeletons in 2004, scientists collected samples of the bones as well as bits of preserved human tissue. They carried out DNA tests that revealed a rather shocking thing—the 300-odd skeletons belonged to two distinct groups of people, for there were evident differences in the bone features of their bodies. And all the remains dated back to the 9th century CE. The first one was a group of short people with thinner, shorter bones. The second group included people who were tall and well-built. The second group outnumbers the first one. Were these two groups related to each other? Scientists believe they were not. A few of these samples have unique DNA, which is not found anywhere in the world but only in a particular group of people from Maharashtra, while a few of them have DNA that has characteristics of the hill people of the Himalayas.

Many anthropologists believe that since Roopkund is almost 35 kilometres away from the nearest human settlement and it would have been impossible for the pilgrims to venture into the area on their own, they employed local people as porters.

The plausible scenario of what could have happened is that the taller group—with people who were related to each other (a large family or a tribe)—probably wanted to make a pilgrimage through the mountain and they hired some local people as guides. Perhaps the two groups met at the foot of the mountain and walked uphill when suddenly, enormous cricket ball-sized hailstones rained down and hit these people on their heads and caused them to die.

A study published in 2019 by a team of Indian and international scientists also suggests that the remains belong not just to Indians but also to people who hailed from Southeast Asia and faraway Greece. The scientists say that they did not die in a single catastrophic event but because of multiple incidents occurring over a thousand years. But they're still not sure what brought these people to Roopkund or how exactly they died!

MAGICAL MUSHROOMS

Some people also believe that the skeletons belong to groups of people who came to the valley in search of magical mushrooms, or 'keeda jadi' in the local language. It's said that every spring, the valley sprouts thousands of these caterpillar fungi, which contain unbelievable medicinal properties. The fungus is highly valuable. Maybe some people headed out in search of them in the springtime and found themselves in the midst of a most devastating natural disaster. The journey could have progressed well until the point everyone was trapped, with no place to run and hide as disaster struck and a violent torrent of hailstones falling from the skies battered the whole group.

Could this be true? Well, your guess is as good as ours!

THE MYSTERY OF THE SKELETON LAKE

Over the years, the Skeleton Lake mystery has teased many historians, anthropologists and archaeologists who have been doggedly looking for answers the world is waiting for: What really happened in Roopkund? Who do these skeletons belong to? What combination of factors led to the death of these people? Why are the wounds on all skeletons only on the heads and the shoulders?

The mysteries surrounding the Roopkund are many but, we guess, the lake is not going to give out its secrets too easily! Whatever may be the case, you should try and visit this mystery lake at least once. Who knows?—maybe you will be the next one to find something strange about this place!

2
A *Monument with No Pillars*
Bara Imambara

The year 1784 might have passed as any other year in the history of Awadh (in present-day Uttar Pradesh) if not for a terrible famine that struck the region that year. So severe were its effects that not only the common people, but even most of the noblemen were reduced to penury. People had no jobs and no food to eat. At that time, the Nawab of Awadh, Asaf-ud-Daulah, came up with a brilliant way of generating employment for the rich and the poor alike. He did not want to give out free doles to jobless workers and believed that people needed to earn a living and not depend on charity, so he decided to build the biggest prayer hall in the country, an imambara. The imambara would need many workers and all the people working on it and their families would be fed by the Nawab. So the Nawab summoned the best architects of the time and commissioned them to design a grand prayer hall. After shortlisting the design created by Kifayatullah, an architect from Shahjahanabad (in present-day Delhi), he laid the foundation of the most ambitious building of the province, the Bara (meaning 'big') Imambara.

The Nawab employed more than 20,000 men for the construction of the complex. Soon, they started their work—digging, laying bricks, carving stone and wood, carrying earth. It is said that the common people would erect the walls during the day, and on every fourth night, the noblemen would bring down whatever was constructed. For their efforts, the nobility also received payments. This ensured that the work lasted and common people did not starve while the unskilled aristocrats were also employed and their much-needed anonymity thoroughly maintained—this was the Nawab's way of making sure that no one in his kingdom was ever out of work. (Yes, quite ingenious and generous this Nawab was!)

ROOF OF RICE HUSKS

Did you know that this royal structure was built without any modern tools and made of organic compounds? Yes, that's true. The walls of the imambara are made from a mixture of urad dal (black grams) and limestone, and the roof is made from rice husk. Tree gum and jaggery were used instead of cement to fix the bricks together. Fascinating, isn't it?

The famine lasted eleven long years. And to continue to generate employment, the construction also continued for the period the famine lasted. Despite the repetitive building and breaking, the Bara Imambara, also called the Asafi Imambara after the Nawab, turned out to be magnificent. It was neither a mosque nor a mausoleum, but was meant to be a prayer hall where the community could congregate for mourning during Muharram. It rivalled Mughal architecture, and even today, the imambara is thronged with crowds who get mystified by the grandeur and exquisiteness of this mega monument.

A PALACE BUILT ON A HUT

It is believed that the place chosen by the Nawab of Awadh to build the Bara Imambara had the hut of an old woman in which she kept a small tazia—a replica of the shrine of Imam Hussain, Prophet Muhammad's grandson. She was reluctant to give her land to the Nawab but when he promised to keep her tazia in the imambara, she gave the land for free. The tazia is kept in the Bara Imambara even today.

INSIDE THE IMAMBARA

The Bara Imambara is a large complex, which has a mosque, courtyards, gateways and a baoli (stepwell) with running water. The main building of the imambara is a three-storeyed building constructed on a raised platform that one can enter through one of the two arched gateways separated by a grassy courtyard. On the left of the main building is the exquisite seven-level Shahi Baoli, initially dug as a well during the construction. As it was a perennial source of water, a guest house was built around it later.

During the days of the nawabs, the heat-stricken citizens of Lucknow went to Shahi Baoli in the summer months for its cool breeze. The baoli is at an angle of 45 degrees to the main gate of the imambara. What's interesting is that it offers a secret view of the visitors! Because of the angle in which it was constructed, and the alignment of one of the windows of the building, the water of the baoli reflects the shadow of the visitors. When the British came to India, the guards of the Nawab could see the red uniforms of the British soldiers at the main gate reflected in the clear water of the baoli—much like the CCTVs that watch over people's gates these days!

On the right side of the main edifice is a flight of stairs that leads to a plinth on which stands the three-domed Asafi mosque. Surrounded by intricate minarets, the mosque has two large prayer halls and eleven arched doors.

The mosque faces Mecca, the holiest city in Islam. It was also built as part of relief measures. With sculptured domes and minarets, the mosque provides a most splendid look and many thousands of people of Lucknow come here on Friday to offer namaz. There's also a story about how a secret tunnel was created in the mosque, which goes all the way to Delhi. It's believed that this secret tunnel was later sealed by the British after some of their soldiers went looking for royal treasure there and never came back.

THE GENIUS ARCHITECT

Kifayatullah, the architect who designed the Bara Imambara, did not take a penny from the Nawab for his services. He only asked for land for his burial as fees. He is buried, along with the Nawab, in the central hall of the Bara Imambara.

LOOK-NO BEAMS!

Even as the architects spent days, weeks and months designing the Bara Imambara and the other buildings in the complex (including the mosque and the stepwells), they were given an interesting challenge by the Nawab to work on. For prayer purposes, it was decided that a big central hall would be built without any columns or pillars! It's a very large structure, and building it by conventional means would have required columns to bear the load of the ceiling, including the mammoth dome. For such a massive structure, the absence of pillars sounded almost impossible. But then the great architect who was working on the imambara had a brainwave and he decided to create eight chambers in such a way that all of them have different roof heights and lend support to each other. The space above and below these chambers is like a magic maze that supports the massive dome on top of the imambara.

This unique architectural design gave birth to the famous Bhul Bhulaiyya, which is a network of narrow passageways that, when negotiated correctly, wind their way to the upper floor, leading eventually to the rooftop balcony. This strange labyrinth has about a thousand passageways and 489 identical doorways. Some passages have dead-ends, some have steep drops and some others lead to the entrance of exit points. Only one passageway leads to the rooftop balcony. If one gets into the labyrinth, it would be easy to get lost in its numerous passageways and it might take a while before one has figured the way out!

Thus, one of the largest existing mazes in India, the Bhul Bhulaiyya, though created for practical purposes, has become the showstopper of the imambara!

THE BIG AND SMALL OF IT

Apart from the Bara Imambara, Lucknow also boasts of a Chhota (small) Imambara. Located around 2 kilometres from the Bara Imambara, the Chhota Imambara is called the Palace of Lights. If the Bara Imambara is about the brilliance of dark, cryptic passageways, then its petite younger cousin is all about light and glitter. This elaborate black-and-white tomb was constructed in 1832 by the third king of Awadh, Mohammed Ali Shah. Decorated with marvellous calligraphy, it has a serene and intimate atmosphere. Mohammed's silver throne and red crown can be seen here, as well as countless chandeliers from Belgium, Paris and China. This imambara looks splendid with all these chandeliers lit during special occasions!

In the garden of the Chhota Imambara is a water tank and two replicas of the Taj Mahal that are the tombs of Nawab Mohammed Ali Shah's daughter and her husband. Outside the complex, there is a salmon-coloured watchtower, known as Satkhanda. It's believed that the Nawab wanted to build a tower similar to the Qutub Minar in Delhi. But its construction was abandoned after the creation of four storeys in 1840 when Nawab Mohammed Ali Shah died.

AN ARCHITECTURAL MARVEL

If the Taj Mahal in Agra is a symbol of love, Lucknow's Bara Imambara is all about empathy and compassion. While its architecture itself—a huge hall with beautifully adorned ceilings and no pillars—inspires wonder, the history associated with it—of Nawab Asaf-ud-Daulah commissioning the imambara during the time of the great famine to enable Awadhis to earn a living, as he thought they would be too proud to takes alms from the Nawab—makes it a fascinating piece of architecture. This is precisely the reason why the centuries-old building is much more than a monument and never fails to generate awe both in the people of Lucknow and the visitors to the city alike. What brought the strange idea to the Nawab is unknown, but his ingenuity and generosity sure led to the creation of a magnificent structure that nobody in the world has ever been able to replicate. During the Nawab's time, there was a popular saying, that if one does not receive something from God then he will receive it from Nawab Asaf-ud-Daulah. And by visiting the imambara, one can see why this saying was prevalent among the people of Lucknow.

HEAR IT OUT!

Inside the main hall of the imambara, the acoustics are such that even a match being struck on the other side of the hall can be heard. Whoever said walls have ears probably said it while visiting the Bara Imambara!

3
The Great Wall of India
Kumbhalgarh Fort

You must have heard about the Great Wall of China—the longest wall in the world, built more than a millennium ago. But what if we told you that one of the longest walls in the world is in India? Yes, that indeed is true. Built in the 15th century, this wall is nestled between thirteen towering mountain peaks in the deserts of Rajasthan and surrounds the ancient fort of Kumbhalgarh, some 80 kilometres from the city of Udaipur.

Extending some 36 kilometres around the perimeter of the Kumbhalgarh Fort on the westerly range of the Aravalli Hills, it snakes through valleys, bearing a striking resemblance to its distant cousin in China. The fort was built by Rana Kumbha, the ruler of the kingdom of Mewar. It is also the birthplace of one of the most revered Rajput kings and the warrior whom the Mughals most feared—Maharana Pratap.

Though the fort in its present state was built by Rana Kumbha, the area was considered to be of high strategic importance long before the Sisodia Dynasty came to power. Historians believe that the very first fort to occupy the spot was built as early as the 3rd century. Back then, it was King Samprati, the grandson of the great Mauryan King Ashoka, who got the fort constructed. At that time, the village around the fort was called Machhind, and so the fort was named Machhindrapur. A majority of historians consider King Samprati a peace-loving and courageous king. He had managed to establish several Jain centres across different Arab countries, including Iran.

STUFF OF LEGENDS

Kumbhalgarh separated the Mewar kingdom from the Marwar kingdom, and was a safe haven in times of war. According to legends, Udai Singh, Rana Kumbha's son, who went on to inherit the throne, was smuggled into the fort as an infant by his nanny, Panna dhai, when Chittorgarh, Mewar's capital, was under siege in 1535. Legends have it that she replaced the prince with her own son, who was killed by the enemy!

It is not very clear though as to what happened in the region or with the site of the fort until the beginning of the 14th century. At that point, Allauddin Khilji occupied the area. He was one of the greatest rulers of the Khilji dynasty, who was running successful campaigns on the Indian subcontinent, acquiring territories of even the southernmost parts of it. He had invaded most of Rajasthan and attacked Mewar incessantly. And so, Rana Kumbha decided to rebuild the fort with a long wall so it could be used as a refuge if the Rajput kings felt vulnerable in their palaces. The wall was also built to separate Mewar from Marwar, which eventually brought prosperity and progress to the region. Unlike the Great Wall of China, which took more than 1,800 years to complete, the Great

Wall of India, as the fortification of Kumbhalgarh Fort is often referred to, took just a little over a decade and a half to finish. In their heydays, the Mewar kings built a chain of fortresses, which spread from the Aravalli mountains in the north, to southern Rajasthan. During his reign, Rana Kumbha is said to have built around thirty-two forts, of which Kumbhalgarh was the largest.

THE GORY STORY

It is said that Rana Kumbha initially wanted to build a fort at Keliwada, which was about 7 kilometres from the present site. But each time the fort wall began to be built, it would collapse midway. Rana Kumbha failed multiple times in constructing the mammoth wall until he went to a saint who suggested the present-day spot for the fort and said a human sacrifice was needed to construct it. (Sounds weird, right? To us, too!) But who would volunteer to be killed? When no one came up for some time, the saint himself volunteered to sacrifice his life. The saint said to Rana Kumbha: 'I'll climb the hill, Rana, and you follow me. The point where I stop first, build the main entrance of the fort there. I'll climb up further and when I stop for the second time, I will sacrifice myself and you build a temple there. Where my body falls, that mark will be the last point of the great wall.' The king agreed reluctantly and walked with the saint right up to the present entrance of the fort and did as was suggested by the saint. Many versions of this story still float around in Rajasthan but nobody knows for sure if the story is true or not!

AN ARCHITECTURAL WONDER

The snake-like wall to the main fort seems to go up endlessly, as if to reach out to the clouds. Then, you see a fort sitting on top of a hill, some 3,600 feet above sea level. Designed by one of the most famous architects of that time, named Mandan, who was also a theorist and author in Rana Kumbha's court, the fort was built with strict adherence to Vastu Shastra, the ancient Hindu system of architecture. The fort has 15-feet-thick frontal walls that house seven gates of which Haathi Pol, Hanuman Pol and Ram Pol are the major gates. ('Pol' in the local language means main gate, by the way).

If you walk to the fort, passing through the different pols, you cannot but marvel at how clever the design of the fort is! There are sharp turns and congested staircases, designed to slow down invaders. There are eyeholes in the battlement that work as binoculars—one can look down at the whole valley and see any approaching enemy! The path on the ramparts is wide enough for eight horses to walk side by side at the same time—built to offer a stronghold in case of an attack. There are strategic spots along the wall that allowed the soldiers a clear view of the Thar Desert and the distant Aravalli Range. And yet, despite its spread and massive structure, it is beautifully hidden between the hills, which speaks a great deal about the brilliant planning and architecture of ancient Indians. Many an enemy must have gone round in circles trying to find where the fort is, as it can only be spotted from a mere 500 metres from any side. Isn't that amazing?

TEMPLES, TEMPLES EVERYWHERE!

The Kumbhalgarh Fort has around 360 temples, of which 300 are Jain temples and the rest are Hindu temples. The reason why there are so many Jain temples could be that the area was ruled by the Mauryan King Samprati at one point of time. There is a Neelkanth Mahadev Temple inside the fort complex with a 5-foot Shivalinga. At the main entrance through the Hanuman Pol of the fort, there's a temple that's believed to have been made to commemorate the sacrifice of the saint.

Built entirely out of sturdy stone blocks more than five centuries ago, the fort has withstood the vagaries of nature and stands tall and strong as if it was built just yesterday! It is indeed an architectural wonder and a testimony of the talents of the architects of that era.

A JOURNEY BACK IN TIME

Inside the double-storeyed fort, there are patches of greenery, open courtyards and terraces. There are also some noteworthy structures such as the king's and queen's chambers, the watchtower, the rainwater reservoirs and the cannon room. There are different sections with rooms constructed inside the fort and given different names like Badal Mahal, Kumbha Mahal, etc. The courtyard is attached to two royal chambers—one each for men and women, both connected with a corridor. The royal kitchen once stood close to these chambers. To feed the thousands of people who lived inside the fort, a giant kitchen was constructed, complete with stone chimneys. Though the kitchen was segregated into two sections for vegetarian and non-vegetarian food, the fact that both kinds were cooked under the same roof is an instance of harmony and tolerance that could be inspirational today.

Kumbhalgarh Fort has some five ancient cannons on display in a special section called the top khana (a room for cannons), which give a glimpse of the scale and grandeur of the Rana's armoury during the fort's heydays. It is said that Rana Kumbha used to light giant lamps, which used 100 kilogrammes cotton and 50 kilogrammes pure ghee, to provide light to the farmers working at night. The lamps used to glow so brightly that their brightness would reach across miles.

A PALACE OF CLOUDS

The fort's highest point is the Badal Mahal, or Palace of Clouds. It's a room where the king and queen are said to have caught up over a good view of the hills. From the window of the Badal Mahal, it feels as if the clouds are flying right above your head.

This room gives almost a bird's-eye view of the fort and the Aravalli Range, winding out to the horizon for as far as one's eyes can follow. Certain sections have beautiful elephant carvings, painted in natural colours. It is from this spot that the portion of the wall that separates Mewar from Marwar can be seen.

Inside the fort, you cannot help but imagine the hustle and bustle a few centuries ago—the thriving structure, the luxurious excesses, how courageous soldiers must have stood guard in the watchtower... It is as though Rana Kumbha left behind the structure to give us a peep into the times he lived in!

AN ALMOST INVINCIBLE FORT

Counted as one of the most invincible forts in India, the Kumbhalgarh Fort must have been a tough challenge for the invading armies in the medieval era—and it must have left them wondering how to breach the famed and impregnable wall of the fort!

The fort remained almost invincible throughout the Mewar rulers' era. It took the combined forces of Emperor Akbar, Raja Uday Singh of Marwar, Raja Man Singh of Amer, the Mirzas of Gujarat and a water crisis, for the fort to finally be invaded. The invaders poisoned the fort's source of drinking water and the Rajputs had to surrender due to a shortage of water. Shahbaz Khan, a general of Emperor Akbar, took control of the fort in the late 1500s. In 1818, the Marathas took over the fort.

There's something indomitable about a fort's seemingly endless walls—most of which stretch from hill to hill, like a huge anaconda waiting to spring into action. While most Indian forts are either on hilltop vantage points or in the midst of some forest as a protective cover, the Kumbhalgarh Fort has both. It stretches across a hill range, giving a clear line of vision for miles away; it also lies in the heart of what is now a wildlife sanctuary. Kumbhalgarh Fort, along with five other forts of Rajasthan, was declared a UNESCO World Heritage Site under the group 'Hill Forts of Rajasthan' in 2013.

Call it strategic inaccessibility, revolutionary design or nature's mercy, the Kumbhalgarh Fort remains one of the strongest forts of India and bears testimony to the genius and splendour of war tactics and the architectural finesse of people who lived long, long ago...

4
A Tree or a Monument?
The Great Banyan Tree

*O*n a hot summer day, when the roads are all roasted by the sun, when the water loses its cool and the air is heavy, and when not a single bird dares to fly out of its shady nest, there is nothing quite like sitting idly under the cool, dense canopy of a large banyan tree. It is like a sigh of relief—supporting numerous birds in its body and many weary travellers under its shade.

There are numerous banyan trees in India—from ancient to quite young—but there's this one banyan tree that holds a special place among all the banyan trees across the country: It's the Great Banyan Tree in Acharya Jagadish Chandra Bose Indian Botanic Garden in Kolkata, on the west bank of Hooghly River in Shibpur, Howrah. At more than 255 years of age, it is one of the oldest citizens of the city and amongst the widest trees in the world. This gigantic tree, with a circumference of approximately 450 metres and a spread of about 4 acres, is as large as many forests and has even made its way to the Guinness World Records. So what is it really: A tree? A dense jungle? A canopy? A natural wonder? Or a monument? Well, it's all this and more. Let's read how!

WHAT'S IN A NAME?

How do you think the banyan tree got its name? The story goes that banyan trees used to be very popular in villages because people gathered and met under the shade of the huge tree. It happened to be the most favourite meeting place of the merchant class (called bania) and they sat there for hours, discussing business deals. So, the tree came to be named after them.

The scientific name of the banyan is Ficus benghalensis, and it grows widely throughout tropical Asia. It is an evergreen tree. Its leaves are large and heart-shaped and it bears a fig-like fruit that's bright red in colour. Although unfit for human consumption, birds and monkeys eat the fruit of the banyan. The leaves are used as fodder for animals. The tree grows to a height of several metres—21 or more—and lives for many, many years. When the original trunk grows old and faces decay, the tree is supported by the younger ones. That is why the banyan tree is said to symbolize eternal life. It is also called kalpavriksha, or the tree that fulfils all wishes, and is considered sacred by many.

THE TALE OF A TREE

The Indian Botanical Garden, which was called Royal Botanic Garden or Company Bagan ('bagan' means garden in Bengali) during the British Raj, and was renamed the Acharya Jagadish Chandra Bose Indian Botanic Garden in 2009 in honour of the great polymath and natural scientist, is home to the grand old banyan tree. The garden was first proposed to be established in 1786, during the time of the East India Company, at the suggestion of Colonel Robert Kyd who was an amateur botanist and secretary to the board in the military department of Fort William. But Kyd envisioned a garden mainly as a centre where plants with potential commercial value could be identified and grown. Kyd had been able to get a large area of about 330 acres for the garden, which was 6 kilometres downstream of Hooghly River, on the opposite side of Calcutta (present-day Kolkata). But before he could bring in the entire area into cultivation, he died. It was Kyd's successor, William Roxburgh, who brought order to the garden and expanded it. He had great knowledge of European botanical gardens and had spent a considerable time studying and documenting the plants in southern India. He was the first salaried superintendent of the botanical garden and, during his twenty-year-long tenure, drew up a systematic account of the plants in India. He classified a large number of plants previously unknown. Under him, the botanical gardens flourished and many different kinds of plants were brought in from across the world. When he first joined the Botanic Garden, there were some 300 different types of plants, but by the time he left, there were over 3,000. He also wrote a one-of-a-kind book on India's botanical heritage, called *Flora Indica* (Descriptions of Indian Plants). It had an exhaustive listing of all the plants found in India and for over a century after it was written, it served as the basis of subsequent botanical study in India, earning Roxburgh the title of 'The Father of Indian Botany.'

IN CULTURE AND MYTHOLOGY

In Indian culture, banyan trees are among the most revered. The banyan is considered to be a sacred tree in various religions; for example, in Hinduism, it symbolizes longevity and represents the divine creator, Brahma, and in Buddhism, it is significant because it is believed that Buddha sat beneath one for seven days after achieving enlightenment.

Roxburgh decided to live in the garden and he built a large house by the river to accommodate his family. The house still exists, although dilapidated, and has acted as one of the major attractions of the garden.

Though the Botanic Garden has been there in Kolkata since 1787, legend has it that the Great Banyan Tree had been there even before. Though there's no official record of when it came to life, many believe that it was born when the seeds of a banyan tree were carried by a bird that dropped it on top of a phoenix (date palm) tree. The seeds, nourished by the moisture and warmth within the palm tree, quickly sprouted and grew small branches. These branches grew long aerial roots that reached downwards eagerly towards the ground. Once these grasping roots reached the ground and got a firm grip in the earth, they enlarged to become strong trunks that wrapped themselves firmly around the trunk of the palm tree. The strong roots of the Banyan Tree strangulated the date palm tree, which gradually stopped growing and died much before the botanical garden was established.

A TREE WITHOUT A TRUNK

Just like our great ancestors, the Great Banyan Tree has also seen and been through a lot over the years. Not only has it survived two major cyclones in 1864 and 1867, but its main trunk was also infected with a deadly, wood-rotting fungus after it was struck by lightning in 1925. This infection meant that the Great Banyan's 51-foot-wide main trunk needed to be removed to keep the remainder of the tree healthy. Despite going through such a major surgery, the Great Banyan Tree proved resilient and continues to thrive—it has grown over 2 acres in the last thirty years! Yes—believe it or not—this ever-growing tree stands tall and wide without a trunk! This is thanks to thousands of aerial roots that grow from the tree's branches and go into the ground. This is what gives the impression of a full forest rather than a single tree. The tree spans more than 14,493 square metres and covers an area that's more than the area of an average cricket field! Now that's one strong tree, don't you think?

At the centre of the core area of the Great Banyan Tree, there's also an installation in memory of the lost trunk!

A FOREST OF ITS OWN

If you were to see the Great Banyan Tree in the Acharya Jagadish Chandra Bose Indian Botanic Garden from a distance, you would easily mistake it for a dense forest. But once in, you'd figure out that it's just one tree with many prop roots that have a semblance to trees themselves. (In case you're wondering what prop roots are, they are those roots of the tree that grow from the twigs and stems to the ground to build a strong support system.) A wonder of the plant kingdom, the circumference of the canopy is about 450 metres, which makes it look like a miniature forest. During the first census conducted in 1850, the tree had eighty-nine prop roots and the total canopy circumference was 240 metres. As of now, the tree has 3,772 prop roots, the canopy circumference has increased to 486 metres and the height of the tree is 24.5 metres.

Other Attractions

Even though the Great Banyan Tree is the star attraction of the Acharya Jagadish Chandra Bose Indian Botanic Gardens, there are many other trees there from various regions of India and also from other countries. Trees of the rarest kinds, from Nepal, Brazil, Malaysia (Penang), and Indonesia (Java and Sumatra) can be found here. There are towering mahogany trees, an avenue of Cuban palms and an Orchid House. Mango and tamarind trees shade the grassy lawns. Some of the prized possessions of this garden include twenty-six species of bamboo, 140 cultivars of bougainvillea, 109 species of palm, several screw pines and a splendid collection of cacti.

You'd be surprised to know that there's also a 'mad tree' in the Botanic Garden, none of whose leaves are similar in size or shape! Experts describe the tree as not only crazy but also a symbol of 'unity in diversity', the essence of Indian culture.

The Botanic Garden is also home to many animals and birds. Several birds like the jungle babbler, the golden oriole, the black-rumped flameback, rufous treepie, common drongo and the green bee-eater, live within the boundaries of the garden. Squirrels and mongoose can also be seen scurrying here and there. Other creatures that can be spotted here are signature spiders, snails, butterflies and grasshoppers.

A WALKING-ER-GROWING TREE

Would you believe us if we told you that the Great Banyan Tree is walking? It indeed is—yes, even at the ripe age of 225+! With the prop roots as its legs, the Great Banyan Tree is heading eastwards, following the direction of the sunlight. The long tail-like branches have grown immensely and are seen shifting and drifting away from the original trunk at quite a good distance. Although this change is gradual, it is a remarkable one. The western side of the tree is a boundary of the garden, beyond which are residential buildings and a busy road and the tree has curiously avoided moving towards pollution!

In 1985, when the tree covered an area of 3 acres, a fence was installed around it. But the tree soon outgrew it, crossing the metalled road surrounding it and moving towards the east steadily. The metalled road was then done away with so that the prop roots could get firmly fixed to the ground and a second boundary was built in 2015 around this super-energetic senior citizen. But looking at the health of the tree, the botanists are sure that the tree will soon outgrow the second one too. Considering its robust growth, the Botanical Survey of India, which is the guardian of the Botanic Garden, has nicknamed the Great Banyan Tree 'The Walking Tree'!

THE LIVING LEGEND

Just as great people are often the most gentle, big trees are often the most friendly—and the Great Banyan Tree only proves this to be true. This tree has created its own ecosystem over the years. It is home to over eighty-nine species of birds, along with a large number of animals. Apart from weary travellers and enthusiastic tourists, it attracts a large number of visitor-birds, squirrels, insects and flying foxes, and many of these interesting creatures actually live in the tree, which is full of dark, private corners suitable for a variety of tenants. The banyan is rather like a large housing colony in which a number of different families live next door to each other without interfering very much in each other's businesses!

The greatness of the Great Banyan Tree teaches us generosity, standing high above our heads eloquently. It illustrates just how small we are in this big, beautiful world. And it reminds us of our connection to the earth, and of all the nature around us. It is impossible to do justice to the Great Banyan Tree in just one chapter; but lest the Grand Old Tree be offended, let us promise to plant more trees of all kinds, whenever and wherever possible.

The Care and Keeping of The Great Banyan Tree

Just imagine how complicated it must be to take care of such a massive tree! How many people do you think it takes to do this? Well, it takes a thirteen-member team—four botanists and nine gardeners! The team ensures that the tree stays healthy. They check every inch of the tree to make sure there are no signs of fungal infection or termite infestation. But their biggest job is to help the tree grow its prop roots and 'train' them to grow correctly. Since the tree doesn't have a main trunk, its weight is supported by the prop roots. Also the growth of the tree is on one side, so the team has to be careful about the balance of the tree as well. They do that by making bamboo channels and putting fertilizers in them. They then direct the tender prop roots into the bamboo channels positioned at such an angle that it can support the overhead branch. Soon the prop roots grow and attach themselves to the ground, supporting the branch, and the bamboo channels are discarded.

Do you know that the Great Banyan Tree is India's most glorious natural heritage that will be treasured forever? It is among the most photographed trees of India. The great Japanese filmmaker Akira Kurosawa compared the Great Banyan Tree to the work of the legendary filmmaker, Satyajit Ray, who lived in Kolkata—calling the tree 'miraculously brilliant'. The Government of India also released a postage stamp featuring the Great Banyan Tree in 1987.

5
The Mini Taj
Bibi Ka Maqbara

It is one of the world's most renowned monuments and a magnet to countless tourists from all around the world who visit it each year. Built some 400 years ago, it is a milestone in the architectural history of India. It's grand and magnificent (think, poetry frozen in time), a great symbol of love built by the Mughal Emperor Shah Jahan in the memory of his beloved wife Mumtaz Mahal. We are, of course, talking about the Taj Mahal. And there's no Taj Mahal but Taj Mahal!

Or is there?

Well... surprise, surprise! There's a mini Taj Mahal in Aurangabad in Maharashtra—quite far away from its world-famous, widely celebrated cousin in Agra. It might be known as a clone of the Taj, but there's much, much more to this monument. Tucked between the lofty Sihyachal ranges of the Deccan plateau, Bibi Ka Maqbara, or Tomb of the Lady, stands gracefully on the road between Daulatabad and Aurangabad. Just like the Taj Mahal, it was also built in the memory of a Mughal queen. Do you want to know who? Read on to find out!

WHO WAS 'BIBI'?

Commissioned in 1660 by Mughal Emperor Aurangzeb, Bibi Ka Maqbara was erected in memory of his wife, Dilras Banu Begum, known as Bibi, or a woman of nobility, by her son Azam Shah. After her death, Dilras Banu Begum was given the title of Rabia-ud-Durrani (Rabia of the Age), after an Iraqi noble lady, Rabia Basri, who was known for her benevolence.

THE WONDER OF WONDERS: TAJ MAHAL

Shah Jahan, the fifth Mughal emperor, was a happy king, and his kingdom was most prosperous. He was quite wealthy and so he built many mosques and palaces across the country. But in the fourth year of Shah Jahan's reign, a tragedy struck his kingdom. While he was away, his wife Mumtaz Mahal died giving birth to their fourteenth child. This left the king devastated. He shut himself up in a dark chamber for two long years. Then suddenly, one day, he decided to build a beautiful monument in the memory of his wife, a structure that had never been built before and would never be built again. And the structure came to be the great Taj Mahal!

The story of Dilras Banu is almost like a fairy tale. She was born in the royal family of Iran and was the daughter of Shahnawaz Khan, who was the then viceroy of the state of Gujarat. She married Aurangzeb in 1637 and became his first wife. History says that Aurangzeb and Dilras Banu's wedding was one of the most extravagant and astounding weddings of all time. They had five children and after delivering her fifth child, Dilras died—uncannily enough, just like her mother-in-law and Aurangzeb's mother, Mumtaz Mahal. Both Aurangzeb and his eldest son Azam Shah were grief-stricken and went into mourning. For months altogether, they neither appeared in public nor administered the affairs of the state. It took great efforts for them to come out of their loss. It was in 1660, three years after she passed away, that Aurangzeb decided to build a mausoleum for his wife, on the lines of the Taj Mahal—the great monument that Aurangzeb's father had built.

HELLO, HISTORY!

If you know your history, you'd probably know that Aurangzeb was the sixth Mughal emperor of India. But if you find it difficult to remember the names of all the Mughal emperors in the right order, here's an easy trick to remember the first seven! Just remember:

Buffaloes Have A Juicy Salad And Melons!

Babur → Humayun → Akbar → Jahangir → Shah Jahan → Aurangzeb → Muhammad Azam Shah

A SPITTING IMAGE OF THE TAJ

Who shrunk the Taj Mahal? That's the first thought that comes to mind on spotting Bibi Ka Maqbara, which is almost half the size of the Taj Mahal in Agra. It draws its inspiration from the famous Taj Mahal of Agra and was conceived by Attaullah Rashidi, one of the three sons of Ustad Ahmad Lahori, the chief architect and the mastermind behind the Taj Mahal, who had been given the title of Nadir-ul-Asar (A Rare Gem of the Period) by Shah Jahan himself. Attaullah had apprenticed under his father while he was working on the Taj Mahal and had gathered valuable experience. He was an expert in metal designing and also knew Sanskrit and Persian. In fact, he translated a book by Bhaskaracharya (the great Indian mathematician and astronomer) on mathematics from Sanskrit to Persian. Attaullah was helped by Hanspat Rai, an expert on construction material and its use. Both Attaullah and Hanspat oversaw the construction of the entire structure.

But unlike his father Ahmad Lahori, Attaullah had to work on the structure on a shoestring budget given to him by Aurangzeb. According to inscriptions on the southern gate of the structure, the project cost was ₹665,283 and 7 annas (a currency unit formerly used in India and Pakistan, which is equal to one-sixteenth of a rupee), while the Taj Mahal was built on a lavish budget of ₹32 million at that time. This clearly shows that Bibi Ka Maqbara was a more budgeted exercise than the Taj Mahal. And quite obviously so...for Prince Azam was not Shah Jahan, neither in power nor in riches. Considered to be the golden age of the Mughal Empire, Shah Jahan's reign was a prosperous one. Emeralds, sapphires, rubies, diamonds and all sorts of precious stones were mined from Indian soil during his time and his coffers had been bursting with riches, allowing him to commission the most spectacular examples of Mughal architecture.

Azam Shah, however, lacked the treasury his grandfather had access to, as well as the skilled labour that big money could buy. He had to do with whatever money was doled out to him grudgingly by his penny-pinching father Aurangzeb, who was known for his austere lifestyle and tightfistedness, quite unlike the opulence that characterized his predecessors. Aurangzeb had little interest in architecture and was not at all in favour of building a monument as lavish as the Taj. But Aurangzeb's son Azam was determined to have a monument to his mother's name that might vie with the Taj. Somehow, Azam Shah pursued his father, who eventually relented. And the maqbara, or the mausoleum, was completed in about a decade of the Begum's death (unlike the twenty-odd years that the Taj Mahal took).

CAN A MONUMENT BE RELOCATED?

A story goes that, in 1803, Nizam Sikander Jah annexed Aurangabad to his kingdom and was so captivated by Bibi Ka Maqbara that he wanted to relocate the mausoleum to the capital city of his kingdom, Hyderabad. He even ordered his men to dismantle the structure, slab by slab. But then, he had a premonition that if he shifts the structure, some disaster might befall him. He stopped the work, and as a penance, got a mosque built, which still stands to the west of the main structure.

SAME SAME, BUT DIFFERENT

Bibi Ka Maqbara stands at the centre of an enclosed space which is 458 metres by 275 metres. It has ponds, fountains, water channels and broad pathways. Bibi's mausoleum is built on a raised square platform with four minarets at its corners and stairs on three sides, which lead to the tomb, exactly like in the Taj Mahal. The Mughal architects laid great importance on having a river or a stream pass through the monuments they erected, and Bibi Ka Maqbara is no different. Just like the free-flowing Yamuna River

The Mini Taj

was an integral part of the design of the Taj Mahal, the Kham River, which originates from the Lakenvara Hills in the Satara mountain range of Maharashtra, flows behind Bibi Ka Maqbara. It also has a charbagh-style garden and a pavilion with twelve doors to allow the free flow of air—both of which are common features in Mughal architecture. The pathways are decorated with trees on both the sides. There is a water pool and the centre of the pathway consists of fountains and broad reservoirs. To the west of the mausoleum is a mosque and facing the east is Aina Khana, or the mirror chamber, which has mirrors fixed on its doorway.

The Taj has been constructed completely in marble; even its entrance structure, which is made of red sandstone, is interspersed with marble. But Bibi Ka Maqbara—except for the small central portion of the main mausoleum and the dome—is constructed in red sandstone, lime and stucco plaster—the reason why the walls of the Maqbara are a little dusky as compared to the Taj.

Bibi Ka Maqbara also has an onion dome, just like the crowning glory of the Taj Mahal, but the dome of the maqbara is smaller than the dome of the Taj. The white dome of the maqbara has panels adorned with intricate designs of flowers. However, these drawings are quite different from those in Taj Mahal. At the centre of the mausoleum is a humble grave surrounded by an octagonal lattice screen of white marble. But the mausoleum doesn't boast of semi-precious stones inlaid in the design, or gold plating—riches that once lured raiders to the Taj.

Whatever the differences and similarities between the Taj and Bibi Ka Maqbara, each of the two monuments has its own grace and charm. Though Bibi Ka Maqbara looks strikingly like the Taj, it is a pleasant construction by itself. Surrounded by a colourful garden, with tall cypress trees, huge mango trees, and colourful rose bushes and seasonal flowers, it gives a beautiful view of the city. And what adds to its glory is that it is the only monument erected by the Mughals in the Deccan and, hence, is also referred to as the Taj of the Deccan.

WAH TAJ!

When Shah Jahan built the Taj Mahal, his resolve must have been to create a building that had never been created before and one that no one would be able to copy (perhaps that's why a legend goes that Shah Jahan chopped off the hands of all those who worked on the Taj!). Though it's true that nothing can beat the magnificence of the Taj Mahal, there are quite a number of replicas of the Taj Mahal in India! Don't believe us? Well, read on about some of these replicas and you might just change your mind...

Bulandshahr, Uttar Pradesh

Did you know that there's a Taj Mahal in Bulandshahr as well? The story behind it is truly adorable. It is believed that retired postmaster Faizul Hasan Qadri spent all his savings to build a replica of Taj Mahal in the memory of his wife. It is known as the Mini Taj Mahal of Bulandshahr in Uttar Pradesh.

Junagarh, Gujarat

The Nawab of Junagarh built a palace-mausoleum in the 18th century, which looks somewhat like the Taj Mahal. It blends the elements of Islamic, Hindu and European architecture and is known as Mahabat Maqbara.

Lucknow, Uttar Pradesh

There's a small mausoleum that lies inside the Chhota Imambara complex in Lucknow, and it is quite a lookalike of the Taj Mahal. It's called Shahzadi Ka Maqbara and inside the tomb are the buried remains of Princess Zinat Asiya, daughter of King Mohammad Ali Shah Bahadur, the third emperor of Awadh.

Agra, Uttar Pradesh

Yes, there's one more 'Taj Mahal' in Agra. It's called the Red Taj. It is a tomb of a Dutch soldier, John William Hessing, constructed by his wife Ann Hessing. It is not as big or grand as it lacks the lavish marblework of the original Taj but carries a moving tale that makes it worth a visit.

Kolkata, West Bengal

This, we're sure, you'll be surprised to know—the inspiration of the famous Victoria Memorial in Kolkata was also the Taj Mahal! Often called the 'Taj Mahal of the East', Victoria

Memorial was built in the memory of Queen Victoria and was thought up by Lord Curzon, the viceroy of British India. He was awestruck when he first saw the Taj Mahal and he wanted to build a similar memorial structure upon Queen Victoria's death. White Makrana marble was used in the construction of the Victoria Memorial Hall, just like in Taj Mahal. The dome and other structural elements also echo the design of Taj Mahal. The huge gardens surrounding the memorial were also inspired by the Char Bagh of the Taj. It took nearly sixteen years to complete and was inaugurated in 1921.

THE INSPIRATION BEHIND THE TAJ

Now, we know that the Taj has inspired a bevy of structures. But do you know which structure inspired the Taj? The Humayun's Tomb in Delhi! Commissioned by Mughal Emperor Humayun's wife, Hamida Banu, in 1565, in the memory of her husband, it was the first garden-tomb in India. Though it is built in red sandstone, the structure looks similar to the Taj Mahal and it's believed that it inspired several major architectural innovations that culminated in the design of the Taj Mahal.

THE TAJ AND THE MINI TAJ

Though separated by time, magnitude and distance, the Taj and the Mini Taj (aka Bibi Ka Maqbara) are related to each other in more ways than one. Both Taj Mahal and Bibi Ka Maqbara are great symbols of love and loss. While the first memorial, Taj Mahal, was built by Shah Jahan for his beloved wife and Aurangzeb's mother, Mumtaz Mahal; the second, Bibi Ka Maqbara, was built by Aurangzeb and his son Azam Shah in the memory of Aurangzeb's wife and Azam's mother, Dilras Banu—two gracious ladies who were known for their generosity, kindness and charitable nature, immortalizing them in the chapters of history...

6

The Lake that Casts Moon Magic

Lonar Crater Lake

*D*o you ever look at a shooting star and make a wish? If you know your science, you'd know that shooting stars are actually meteors or broken pieces of celestial bodies such as asteroids and comets that enter the earth's atmosphere. Most of them burn off, but occasionally a large one hits the earth's surface—exactly what happened more than 40,000 years ago! A huge, blazing ball of fire, which weighed between a whopping 1 and 2 million tons, hurtled through space at an awesome speed of 80,000 to 90,000 kilometres per hour. It crashed into earth and hit its surface so hard and with such fiery force that it made a deep depression in the rock-solid Deccan plateau in the heart of Maharashtra. It crashed and exploded—imagine the BANG it would have caused! It then erupted and spewed molten rock, creating a magnificent trough. Even though it was a mere chip of the moon, the impact of the 384,403-kilometre travel from the moon to the earth, left a dent that was 1.8-kilometre wide and 150-metre deep. Over time, the jungle took over, and a perennial stream transformed the crater into a tranquil, emerald-green natural lake—the Lonar Crater Lake.

It does sound like the stuff of sci-fi, but it's true! Every year, between 30,000 and 1,50,000 meteors plunge towards the earth, but none of them have managed to create a lake like Lonar. If you look at the Lonar Lake, it might look like just another lake, but this near-perfect oval lake is one of the world's only two natural craters formed entirely from basalt—a dark, fine-grained volcanic rock—

and has water that is seven-times saltier than seawater! Well, that's the thing about most mysterious places—they wear a nondescript garb and appear pretty ordinary at first glance but when you really start looking at them, you find a million secrets lurking around them. What are the secrets of the Lonar Crater Lake? Let's find out!

> ### THE LITTLE LONAR
>
> *About 700 metres away from the rim of the Lonar Crater, there's a small circular depression that resembles the main crater in its shape and characteristics. It is believed to have originated from the impact of a smaller piece of the meteor that hit the earth, and had split from its main body. The diameter of this crater is 340 metres and it rises 6 metres above ground level. This crater is known as the Little Lonar or Amber Lonar.*

A Mix of Mystery and Mythology

Rimmed by lush green forests and really old temples, the Lonar Crater is straight out of a sci-fi-meets-history-meets-mythology flick. The history of the grove of temples around the Lonar Crater can be traced back to between the 6th and the 12th centuries. Most of these temples and monuments are now in ruins but one can imagine how beautiful they must have once been by looking at their fine architecture. There's a Daitya Sudan Temple in a nearby village that's believed to be the origin of the legend of Lonar. The Puranas (ancient Hindu texts) say that long, long ago, a demon called Lavanasura ('lavana' means salt and 'asura' means demon, in Sanskrit) used to terrorize the villagers here. Lord Vishnu took it upon himself to eliminate this asura from the face of the earth. So he took the form of Daitya Sudan (Killer of a Demon) and went to kill Lavanasura. The demon got so scared that he hid in a lake covered by a hill. Lord Vishnu kicked the hill away and placed his foot on the demon's navel. He pressed it so hard that blood came pouring out of the demon's body and he died. It's believed that the crater symbolizes the demon's navel, the shore his body and the salty water of the lake his blood. Quite a story it is, don't you think? Inside the Daitya Sudan Temple, there's a 4-foot-tall idol of Lord Vishnu and a small painting on top of the ceiling shows the deity crushing the asura with his foot. There are many other temples on the banks of the Lonar Crater Lake, like Kamalja Devi Temple, Mora Mahadev Temple, Hanuman Temple and Munglyacha Temple.

The Lonar Crater Lake finds a mention in the Ramayana as well, where it's called Panchapsar Sarovar. The story goes that a great sage named Mandakarni stayed under the waters of this lake for 10,000 years. Lord Indra, threatened by the sage's long penance, sent five beautiful apsaras *(celestial nymphs) to distract him. The apsaras ended up becoming the sage's wives, and the lake came to be known as Panchapsarotataka, or the Lake of Five Nymphs!*

And that's not all—the salty waters of the lake are also written about in Ain-i-Akbari, the chronicles of the Mughal Emperor Akbar, penned by his close friend and adviser Abu'l Fazl in 1590 CE. *He writes that the hills around the crater produce all the requisites for making soaps and glass, which yielded considerable revenues for the Mughal Empire during Akbar's time. He also mentions that on these hills is a lake of saltwater, but the water from the centre and the edges is perfectly fresh.*

THE CHANCE DISCOVERY

For a long time, Lonar Crater was one of the best-kept secrets of Maharashtra. Though it is only about 170 kilometres from Aurangabad and 550 kilometres from Mumbai, it remained unknown to everyone. Since the path towards the lake was slippery and people believed its banks to be quicksand swamps, no one attempted to go near it, for it was a truly treacherous trek. It was only in 1823—some 196 years ago—when a British explorer, J.E. Alexander, chanced upon the crater while he was researching the ancient temples in the region. He found many temples in a dilapidated condition and a strange ecology in this cavernous region, which was very different from the surrounding flat landscape. But even after the discovery of the crater, for almost a century and a half, scientists believed it to be a volcanic crater, for it was found on the Deccan plateau, which is famous for its volcanic origin. Then, in 1896, the famous geologist, G.K. Gilbert, pointed out its similarity with a crater created by a meteor in Arizona desert in the US. Some other scientists too doubted the volcanic theory because of lack of recent volcanic activities in the Indian subcontinent and agreed with Gilbert's theory of a meteoritic origin of Lonar Crater. And so, a scientific debate started: Is Lonar Crater a volcanic or a meteoritic crater?

In 1961, two Indian scientists, N.C. Nandy and V.B. Deo, made a thorough survey of the crater site and came to the most plausible explanation that Lonar Crater was the result of a single violent explosion and began to suspect that it stemmed from an extraterrestrial encounter. And finally, in 1964, two American marine scientists, Eugene C. Lafond and Robert S. Dietz, conducted a field survey at Lonar and suggested that the crater must have been an impact crater and originated some 50,000 years ago. The reasons for their suggesting this were these: First, they found that the crater is circular and has a depth-to-diameter ratio that is characteristic of an impact crater. Second, the crater has a raised rim that could be because of the impact origin. Their suspicions were also confirmed after some curious minerals like maskelynite, a type of glass found on meteorites and in craters formed by meteors, was found at the site.

THE SECRETS OF THE LAKE

Scientists have long been puzzled by the strange mysteries surrounding the Lonar Crater. For starters, this unusual bowl has water that is both saline and alkaline, something that's totally unheard of! Scientists say that it is nearly impossible that a lake is alkaline and saline at the same time, so that makes this lake one of a kind. The lake has two distinct regions that never mix—an outer region that's neutral and an inner region that's alkaline, each with its own flora and fauna. (If you don't believe us, then you can carry a litmus paper with yourself, perform some experiments, and let chemistry prove it to you all over again!) What makes it even more exciting is that the alkalinity of the water increases towards the centre and breeds very rare forms of microbial life—the crater basin encompasses a unique ecosystem that cannot be found anywhere else on the planet!

There is also a perennial stream feeding the lake with sweet water but there seems to be no apparent outlet for the lake's water. And it's also a big unsolved mystery where the water for the perennial stream comes from, in a relatively dry region like the Deccan plateau. Even during the peak summers, this stream is perpetually flowing!

A LOONY FACT

The name 'Lonar Crater' comes from the name of a nearby village, Lonar, in the Buldhana district of Maharashtra. What's bizarre is the fact that the name 'Lonar' is akin to the English word 'lunar', which means 'resembling the moon'. What a coincidence!

Another mystery that makes this lake intriguing is the fact that as soon as you reach there, the directional indicators of your compass either stop working or show huge variations. Scientists have long been befuddling over the turbulent behaviour of the compasses in this area and have tried to find a cause but no one could justify the reason. Many theories have been proposed to explain this phenomenon—some scientists say that strange electromagnetic forces interfere with electrical equipment and send compasses haywire. They suggest that objects that come from space are generally more electromagnetic than material that they strike on earth. And since Lonar Crater is a meteor-impact crater, its electromagnetic field is stronger. This is where it gets more interesting. Could this mean that the lake's weird magnetic properties be extraterrestrial in origin?

Another theory suggests that the wide swinging of a compass' needle is due to the excess iron content in the soil.

Wait—could that mean that the soil around the crater will stick to a piece of magnet if we try rolling one on it? Well, we don't know yet! But scientists at NASA and the Geological Survey of India are attempting to find the answers to the compelling questions surrounding the Lonar Crater, like how is the lake alkaline and saline at the same time? How does it support microorganisms rarely found elsewhere on earth? Why do compasses fail to work in certain parts of the crater? And what unusual secrets lie hidden in its very bottom?

THE BOWL OF BIODIVERSITY

Many scientists have called the Lonar Crater a massive bowl of biodiversity. Why? Because apart from the sci-fi mystery it presents, the Lonar Crater is circled by a thick belt of large trees that run around its basin. This belt is formed of concentric circles of different species of trees. The first ring is formed by date palm trees, followed by a circle of tamarind trees, and then comes a belt of babul trees. These concentric circles of trees make one wonder who would have planted them in this manner around the crater so many years ago!

The core of the concentric circles is bound by a belt of bare muddy space. This space is several-hundred-metres broad but has no vegetation because of the high soda content of the water. During the rainy season, this soil drains into the lake, and during summers when evaporation reduces the water level, large quantities of soda are collected.

SNIFF AND SEE

Be warned—if you go near the Lonar Crater Lake, you'll find that the lake has an unpleasant odour—a smell similar to the one of rotten eggs! This is a sign of hydrogen sulphide in the water of the lake. The colour of the lake is green due to the presence of blue-green algae.

The Lonar Crater is also a wildlife sanctuary and a notified Geo-Heritage monument. It is home to a variety of creatures like the gazelle, langur, bat, mongoose, barking deer and chinkara, along with snakes, scorpions, monitor lizards and brilliantly coloured insects and amphibians. Its other residents include the egret, shelduck, Brahminy duck, red-wattled lapwing, blue jay, baya weaver, hoopoe, barn owl, golden oriole, lark, tailorbird, parakeet, black-winged stilt, green bee-eater, magpie, robin and peafowl, as well as numerous species of migratory birds that often visit the place.

But this unique crater with its fragile ecosystem is under threat. Pollution due to sewage water and human activity in and around the crater is said to be affecting its alkalinity and salinity, thereby threatening its sensitive ecosystem. Excessive water from the lake is being taken for non-agricultural and commercial activities, because of which, experts claim, the lake's surface area has shrunk by a staggering 100 metres in the last three to four years! Deforestation also poses a serious threat to the lake. Some of the streams flowing into the lake have either dried up or have been blocked. It's sad but this bowl of booming diversity is in desperate need of help. It's not every day that nature works in its serendipitous ways to create a spectacular wonder like the Lonar Crater. It has a great importance in geology and astronomy, and we must all come together in conserving it.

THE CURIOUS CASE OF A CRATER

Our universe is an incredible place—with zipping comets, big black holes, stellar bodies and space debris like asteroids and meteoroids. They range from the size of dust particles to those spanning kilometres and weighing millions of tons. Every day, many of these pass within striking distance to our blue planet, which seems to play dodgeball with them. But sometimes, they make contact with the earth, explode and make holes on its surface, changing its very topography. Lonar Crater is one such example of a celestial episode that took place thousands and thousands of years ago. A one-of-a-kind phenomena, it's a geological, geographical, historical, mythical, archaeological, ecological and scientific wonder—all rolled into one. It's a mystery that scientists are trying to unravel fully, and until that happens, we do not know what amazing secrets lie buried within the bowels of Lonar Lake... Perhaps some ancient, extraterrestrial treasure that holds the answers to the mysteries of our universe!

7
The Hanging Pillar
Veerabhadra Temple

You have probably heard of Lepakshi saris. The fabulous designs are taken from the exquisite borders of the pillars of a little-known temple about 120 kilometres from Bengaluru, called the Veerabhadra Temple. Every design is unique and quite intricate. Those sculptors must have taken such pride in their work! The Veerabhadra Temple is located in Lepakshi village, Anantapur District, Andhra Pradesh. Since most of the temple happens to be built on a tortoise-shaped rocky hill, the hill is referred to as Kurmasailam, meaning 'Tortoise Hill' in Telugu. The temple is thought by many to have been built between 1530 and 1545 by Virupanna and Veeranna, two ambitious brothers who were governors under the Vijayanagara Empire during the reign of King Achyuta Deva Raya. He was supposed to have been hand-picked by the famous ruler Krishna Deva Raya, who was his older brother, to be his successor. However, there is another school of thought that believes that the temple was built by Sage Agastya.

Replete with idols of Nandi, Shiva, Vishnu, Ganesh, Bhadrakali, etc., the typical Vijayanagara architectural style is very evident all over the temple with its awe-inspiring sculptures and detailed paintings on the walls and ceiling. The sculptures of gods, goddesses, musicians and dancers are similar to what one would find in the more famous Hampi. The various artworks showcase tales from the epics and the Puranas. These include a 24-feet-by-14-feet fresco of the fourteen avatars of Shiva (one of them being

Veerabhadra) on the ceiling. And the deity of course—almost life-sized, armed and fierce, with a garland of skulls! All in all, Lepakshi is a culturally, historically and archaeologically significant village. But there is something here at the temple, which is even better than all of the above, but we'll come to that in a moment...

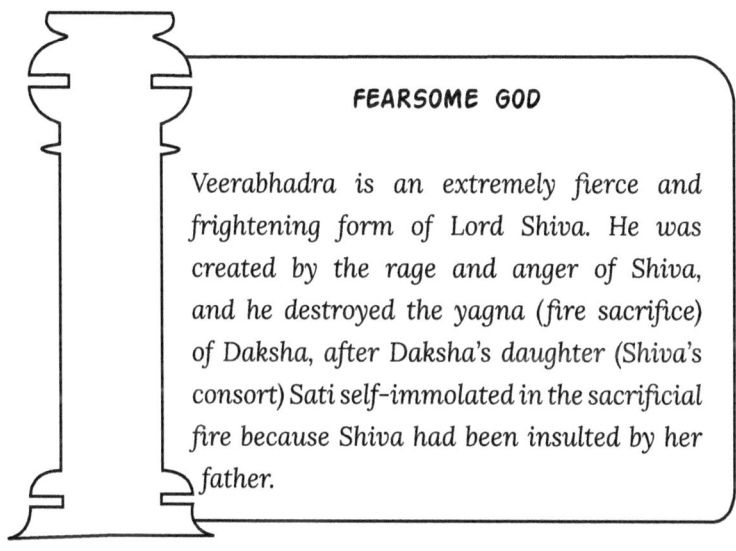

FEARSOME GOD

Veerabhadra is an extremely fierce and frightening form of Lord Shiva. He was created by the rage and anger of Shiva, and he destroyed the yagna (fire sacrifice) of Daksha, after Daksha's daughter (Shiva's consort) Sati self-immolated in the sacrificial fire because Shiva had been insulted by her father.

The Veerabhadra Temple has an open-air Kalyana Mandapam (wedding hall), where the wedding of Shiva and Parvati is believed to have taken place in the presence of other gods and goddesses. But you will notice that the Kalyana Mandapam has been left unfinished. Another local tale says that this venue was supposed to be ready for the wedding of Lord Shiva and Parvati, but since it was not ready, it was not used. And why was it not ready, you might ask. Well, if you look really closely, you will also notice two red spots on the western walls of the temple. According to a local legend, the builder, Virupanna, the treasurer of the Vijayanagara Empire, is believed to have used the money from the treasury to build the temple. Nothing bad about that, is there? But, matters were not so straightforward. This was done when the king was not there! So, when the king returned from his campaign and found that the treasury had been emptied by Virupanna, he was enraged! In his anger, he ordered that the construction be stopped immediately and the treasurer be blinded. So, the wedding hall remained unfinished. As for Virupanna, he could not understand why he was being so severely punished for such a good deed. Angered and upset by this command, Virupanna carried out his punishment himself! So the red blotches on the walls of the unfinished Kalyana Mandapam are supposed to be the blood from his eyes!

Now we come to what is quite a remarkable feature in this temple—something that puts all the other masterpieces in the shade; in fact, something that is an engineering wonder *and* an artistic masterpiece! The outer portion of the temple has a massive dance hall with seventy stone pillars supporting the roof. Did we say seventy? Actually, sixty-nine pillars support the ceiling. One corner pillar is the famous 'hanging pillar' that does not touch the temple floor at all! There is a small gap between the temple floor and base of the pillar and it is possible to pass thin objects such as a sheet of paper or a piece of cloth from one side to the other! If you visit, you'll see many people doing the same thing: putting a piece of cloth or paper underneath and sliding it to the other side, proving that the pillar is disconnected from the floor. How did ancient artisans construct such a huge pillar that defies gravity and hangs from the ceiling? And, we are referring to a 20-foot-tall, solid granite pillar! It would be worth finding out how much it weighs, for we all know that the heavier anything is, the more difficult it is to carry, let alone suspend! And to top it all, the temple, as well as the pillars in the temple, were designed to resist earthquakes!

While there are even more points of interest in the temple, like Durga Paadam, a rock chain, Vastu Purusha, the eyes of Viroopaakshanna, the Padmini race lady, etc., the hanging pillar is the most famous of these attractions. A huge granite Nandi is located about 200 metres from the temple at the front, which is 20 feet in height and 30 feet in length. The statue is decorated with garlands and bells, all carved out of a single block of stone, and is said to be one of the largest of its type in the world. The Nandi statue faces a popular granite statue of a coiled multi-hooded snake in a protective pose over a Shiva Linga on the eastern side of the temple's site.

An inquisitive British engineer had tried to move the pillar. You might wonder why anyone would do that. Well, he wanted to figure out the secret of how it was supported. This occurred in the pre-independence era, by the way. Anyway, during the attempt, ten more pillars also moved!

'RISE, BIRD!'

Incidentally, the name of Lepakshi village has an interesting story to it. The village is regarded as the place where Jatayu fell down after being injured by Ravana. Jatayu is a huge bird in the Ramayana who tried to rescue Sita when Ravana was abducting her. Despite being very old, Jatayu fought very bravely with Ravana but could not stop him. Instead, he was injured during the attempt and fell to the earth. Lord Rama and his brother Lakshmana found the injured and dying Jatayu in their own search for Sita. Before succumbing to his injuries, Jatayu informed them of the fight between him and Ravana and told them that Ravana had gone towards the south. Lord Rama then performed the last rites of Jatayu with full honour. Ramakkalmedu is the place where the last rites were performed. Lord Rama is said to have commanded the bird to rise: 'Le pakshi (Rise, bird)' in Telugu, hence the name of the village and temple.

While analysing this, the engineer realized that every one of the pillars was placed just so, to maintain the balance of the entire structure. And, his operation, if carried through, would result in a distortion of the roof, which would probably make the entire structure collapse! So thankfully, he stopped the operation right away. But not before the magical pillar had got a bit dislodged from its original position.

In another story, it is said that the British government decided to do some repairs and attempted to remove the pillar. But try as they might, they couldn't move it out because it was fixed so perfectly. Not to be deterred, they kept trying and finally managed to only move it barely. They then realized that removing this pillar would be impossible and hence left it in this weird position. All these stories are just hearsay, by the way. Every stone here has a story to tell!

CONCLUSION

With so many theories being put forth regarding this seemingly magical pillar, the story that is really appealing is this: that this miraculous pillar was intentionally built to demonstrate the architectural brilliance of the Vijayanagara builders! What do you think?

8
The Honeycomb Monastery
Phugtal Monastery

If you have visions of a monastery full of honeybee hives after reading the title, think again. There are no bees in this chapter. No hives or honeycombs either! What are being referred to are actually the windows of small, similar-looking constructions that seem like honeycombs from a distance! All these constructions form the elusive Phugtal Monastery, situated high up on a mountain, overlooking the Zanskar Valley. Imagine how the location must have been discovered! One can see why it is believed that sixteen followers of the Buddha were the first occupants of this natural cave—it lies in an obscure corner of the Zanskar Valley, majestically towering over all that it surveys at a height of about 3,800 metres. At this secluded, rarefied spot, it would be so much easier to lead a calm and detached existence, right? Many, many monks followed suit over the centuries, arriving from far and wide, to meditate and lead the simple life in the midst of beauty and serenity in Ladakh. With so many senior monks in residence, student-monks followed them, to learn and benefit from their wisdom. The cave is believed to have been used for about 2,500 years by monks for meditation, way before the monastery was constructed.

THE FOUNDER

Jangsem Sherap Zangpo is believed to have been born in 1395 in the village of Karma in Tibet. At the age of seven, he received vows from Deshin Shekpa, the fifth Karmapa

Lama of the Kagyu School of Tibetan Buddhism, who gave him the name 'Sherap Zangpo'. Je Tsongkhapa was the founder of the Gelug School of Tibetan Buddhism, one of the more modern schools of Tibetan Buddhism. His disciple, Jangsem Sherap Zangpo, set up the present Phugtal Gompa in the early 15th century. Jangsem was first instructed by his mentor to go and spread Buddhism in Ladakh. Sending five more disciples with Jangsem, Je Tsongkhapa gave him a statue of Amitayus to present to the king of Ladakh, requesting for his help in their mission. The statue contained the bone powder and a drop of Je Tsongkhapa's blood. The king was a joyful recipient of the gift and instructed his minister to help Je Tsongkhapa's disciples to set up a monastery in Ladakh. With the king's go-ahead and help, Jangsem and his team set up a monastery called Lhakhang Serpo in Stagmo.

BUDDHA OF LONGEVITY

Amitayus Buddha (Buddha of Limitless Life) holds in his hands the long-life vase, which contains the nectar of immortality. Amitayus is usually shown to be covered with jewels, along with hair that is painted blue at the ends. His elongated earlobes signify his superhuman qualities.

While he is also given credit for establishing the Phugtal Monastery, how that came about is quite fascinating. Three eminent scholars who also happened to be brothers—Dangsong, Pun and Sum—were believed to have the supernatural power of flight! Yes! They imparted teachings on dharma at Phugtal. When Jangsem Sherap Zangpo arrived at Phugtal, the three brothers gave the holy site to him and left. According to legend, the spiritually gifted Zangpo caused a spring to appear and flow from the cave, a tree to grow on top of the cave and for the cave itself to grow larger in size! Then, under his guidance, the structure of the monastery was built around the cave. It is built into the side of the cliff, like a honeycomb. The cliff is part of a lateral gorge of a major tributary of the Lungnak River. Zangpo died in 1457 at the age of sixty-two.

LABOUR OF LOVE

During 1826–27, Sándor Csoma de Kőrös, a Hungarian philologist, stayed at Phugtal Gompa and authored the first English-Tibetan dictionary. In his memory, a stone tablet has been placed.

THE MONASTERY

The name Phugtal (or Phuktal) comes from the words 'Phug', which means cave, and 'tal' or 'thal', meaning 'at leisure'. A second spelling of Phugtal is Phukthar; 'thar' meaning liberation according to the Zangskari dialect of the Tibetan languages. So, what we have is the Cave of Liberation. Today, the Phugtal Monastery houses around eighty monks, a main temple, four prayer rooms, a library, a small clinic, numerous small residential houses, teaching facilities, a kitchen and the original cave with a protected sacred spring. The frescoes in the prayer rooms are similar to the 11th-century ones of Alchi Monastery. The chorten (a Buddhist shrine, typically a saint's tomb or a monument to the Buddha) here is believed to have the relics of its founder, Sherap Zangpo. By the way, the hollow in the rock above the monastery has flowing water that is believed to have mystical healing powers.

The food in the monastery is basic, but well-prepared from scratch by a head cook and his assistants in the kitchen located inside the natural cave. No gas stoves, no oven...very basic cooking equipment is used—just firewood and a few pots. How we get spoilt in the modern world!

Phugtal Monastery is one of the few popular Buddhist monasteries in Ladakh that can be reached only by foot. The supplies to the monastery are brought on horses, donkeys and mules in summer, and in the winter they are transported across the frozen Lungnak River by foot.

The clean waters of the Lungnak River, also known as the Tsarap River, flows to the valley below the Phugtal Gompa.

HISTORY OF THE SCHOOL

Geshe Lharampa Nagri Choszed, a native of Tibet, came to Phugtal in 1959 after the Chinese invasion of Tibet. He also sent out many monks for advance learning to other institutions, who later returned to Phugtal to teach.

'Geshe Lharampa' is the highest Geshe degree conferred within the traditional Tibetan monastic system in the Gelug school. The curriculum requires more than fifteen years of intensive study!

THE VILLAGERS AND THE MONASTERY

Phugtal Monastery has an amchi (Tibetan traditional physician) who provides natural Sowa-Rigpa medicine, prepared at the traditional Tibetan clinic in the monastery. Villagers come to see the amchi when there are health issues. He also visits nearby villages and offers medical assistance to the people in need. The monks from the monastery perform traditional prayers in the village during significant events like births, weddings, deaths, etc. There seems to be an invisible bond between the monks and the villagers.

Geshe Lharampa Nagri Choszed started the Phugtal Monastic School in 1993, with very few children. The demand obviously grew. So, the new Phugtal School was planned and completed in 2014 to provide education for the growing number of children in the Lungnak Valley close by. With no direct access to schools in other parts of Ladakh because of its remote location, the school was a much-needed boon to the villages there. The new campus had a boarding for students coming from further away, quarters for staff to reside in, a library, a kitchen—everything a present-day school should have, opening up the world of knowledge to the children living around the monastery.

Enrolment increased significantly. No fees were charged from the students and the monastery bore the cost of boarding, lodging and study material, with help from sponsors. A lot of the students were children from the local farming families in the Lungnak Valley, who were extremely poor. Complete education was provided, which involved a mix of traditional learning and a modern curriculum for grades 1 to 8. The school had an integrated curriculum that included natural sciences, social sciences, Hindi, English and written Tibetan (Bodhi). It also included traditional Tibetan subjects such as Tibetan Buddhist philosophy and Sowa-Rigpa medicine. As future members of the Phugtal Gompa, the students were trained in all aspects of monastic life too: prayers, rituals, festivals, hymns, etc. The teaching faculty consisted of Geshes, the

Tibetan Buddhist equivalent of a master's degree. There were three Geshes at the school.

But, but...

TRAGEDY STRIKES

On 31 December 2014, a landslide occurred between the Shun and Phugtal villages, which caused a natural dam to form on the Zanskar River. The 10-kilometre-long lake that formed behind the dam slowly increased in length and height without anyone noticing. By the time it was noticed and steps were taken to avoid flash floods, it was too late. On 7 May 2015, the dam burst, the Zanskar River flooded and the entire school campus was washed away! So many years of slow, hard work, gone. The building, equipment, materials and stores were all destroyed. How tragic that the new facility had functioned for barely four months. Fortunately, about forty to fifty families had been moved away, so no lives were lost. But, about six bridges, many, many homes and other buildings were washed away.

NOW WHAT?

Rebuilding is what has been going on ever since the floods in 2015. From scratch! The rebuilding of homes, roads, bridges, and of course, the school. Very, very slowly. The monks of the Phugtal Monastery could do with some help, right? Anyone listening?

FESTIVALS AT THIS GOMPA

Like in all Buddhist monasteries, Phugtal Gompa celebrates Tibetan festivals with gusto. A lot of importance is given to the planning and execution of the traditional customs required for each festival. After all, the festivals give the villagers something to look forward to and emulate, and the monks a chance to mingle with their congregation. Each year, the Phugtal Monastery's calendar of festivals starts around the end of February. The dates of the festivals differ each year.

The festival that commemorates the death anniversary of Je Tsongkhapa, the founder of the Gelug branch of Tibetan Buddhism, is held in early December. It is called Gadam Nagchod, or the Lightning Ceremony.

Monlam Chenmo, the most significant ceremony of the year, is celebrated at the beginning of the new year. Special rituals are performed for the well-being of people and for world peace.

Chonga Chodpa is celebrated just after the Chudsum Chodpa. The monks from Phugtal Monastery make a special statue of their deity from flour and butter, which is worshipped by the villagers.

Gyalwe Jabstan is celebrated after Chonga Chodpa, dedicated to the long life of the fourteenth Dalai Lama.

Some other important ceremonies and festivals are the Jigched Lhachusum and Syungnas.

LONG, LONG JOURNEY

Ready for a donkey ride? Or, maybe a ride on a horse is okay by you? No? Then, walk. For, these are the only three ways to get to the Phugtal Monastery. A few hours' drive from the town of Padum in Zanskar will take you to the road towards the monastery. Newcomers are advised to get properly acclimatized in Padum, a necessity to undertake any high-altitude trek. It takes a tough, arduous trek of two or three days to reach this isolated monastery, which appears to be miraculously glued on to the side of the vertical rock face. There are several inscriptions and stupas (chortens) on the way. Visitors can go through the Padum-Manali trekking route to reach the monastery too. Cha and Anmu are the two villages situated near Phugtal Monastery. Cha is one of the most remote villages in Ladakh. To get there, a drive on paved roads from Leh to Kargil, followed by an equally long journey on unpaved roads to Padum, a town in the Zanskar region, is required.

CHORTENS

Also known more commonly as stupas, there are eight different kinds of chortens. Each marks an important event in the life of the Buddha. The shape of the stupa is a symbol of the Buddha wearing a crown, sitting on a throne.

The landscape of this region of Ladakh looks straight out of an exotic storybook! Trekkers often halt at one of these villages on their journey to Phugtal Gompa. Green patches of land surrounding the two villages show signs of civilization, a stark contrast to the barren landscape on the opposite side. Moonscape is what that kind of terrain is referred to, right? But once there, a visitor gets a unique insight into the lives of Buddhist monks, greeted by humble hosts who are happy to share their healthy food and hot tea. For trekkers or lovers of remarkable architecture, Phugtal Monastery is the place.

9
A Relic of St. Philomena of Italy In India?

St. Philomena's Church

Yes! As you enter Mysuru from the Bengaluru side, there is no way you can miss the magnificent gothic-style church that immediately catches the eye. St. Philomena's Church presents an imposing sight; the perfectly developed portals within the arched entrance and the slim sky-kissing twin spires are overwhelming. This magnificent cathedral, one of the tallest in this country, was built in 1936. Following a neo-gothic style, its distinct stained glass windows and soaring towers could place this site of worship anywhere in the Western world. But this cathedral has a secret that even most residents of Mysuru have no clue about! Even today!

What are the chances of a French statue and relic of a celebrated Greek saint from Italy, finding a place in a cathedral built on the likes of a famous cathedral in Cologne, Germany, and designed by a Frenchman, being located in Mysuru, India? This describes, in short, St. Philomena's Church!

Any of you readers who might have seen the Cologne Cathedral in Germany, or images of it, will see where the designer got his inspiration from. Daly, an artist from France, is believed to have used the cross as the inspiration for the floor plan of St. Philomena's Cathedral.

Although it is known all over the world as St. Philomena's Church or Cathedral, its actual name is the Cathedral of St. Joseph and St. Philomena. More seldom, it is referred to as St. Joseph's Cathedral. With a seating capacity of 800 inside the mail hall, churchgoers can feast their eyes on the exquisite images on the stained glass windows of all the milestones in Christ's life: His birth, the Last Supper, His Crucifixion, His Resurrection and His Ascension. The 175-foot-tall twin spires are an important landmark in the city's landscape.

Initially, over 250 years ago, there was a small church in its place. At that time, Srirangapatna was the capital of Mysore state and many British officers and soldiers used to live there. However, once the capital was changed to Mysore city in 1799, many of them moved to settle in the capital. The small church was too small for the growing congregation, so Maharaja Krishnaraja Wadiyar III earmarked a plot of land on the present Bangaluru-Mysuru road, where a small church was built. In time, that proved inadequate as well, as the city grew.

So plans were made to build a larger church and Maharaja Krishnaraja Wadiyar IV laid the foundation of the new church on 28 October 1933, which was to be built in the place of the small church built by his grandfather. After eight years of construction, the church started functioning in 1941.

SECRET RELIC

The best-kept secret of this cathedral is the relic of St. Philomena from the 3rd century, which is in a beautiful underground catacomb below the main altar, lit with candles in front of the relics of the martyr. The construction of the church was completed under Bishop Rene Fuga's supervision. At that time, Thamboo Chetty, who was the Huzur secretary to the Maharaja of Mysore, obtained a relic of the Saint in 1926 from Italy, and the following year, a new statue of St. Philomena was brought from France. There are a number of churches dedicated to her all over the world. An annual feast is held on 11 August each year in all of them. The remnants of St. Philomena have been preserved in this church even today.

ADAMANT AND DEVOUT LITTLE GIRL

The monarch of Corfu, an island in Greece, had no children. Distraught, he and his wife prayed incessantly for a child and even swore to convert to Christianity if their prayers were answered. The very next year, a daughter was born to them. She was named Philomena, who started showing signs of being very religious from a very young age. Corfu was at that time at loggerheads with Emperor Diocletian who was based in Rome. The Emperor had threatened to declare war against the tiny island. When Philomena turned thirteen, her parents decided to take her to Rome with them when they went to visit Emperor Diocletian to try and make peace with him.

When the Emperor saw Philomena, he was captivated by her beauty and wanted to marry her, much to the relief and pleasure of her parents. This was the only condition he gave them, to stop all aggression against Corfu. Imagine their surprise when Philomena refused! She told her parents very firmly that she had promised to give her life to God. Her refusal made the Emperor furious.

Nothing could make young Philomena accept the offer of marriage—not Diocletian's rage, nor her parents' appeals. She had made up her mind. The Emperor ordered that she should be imprisoned in the dungeons, hoping to make her change her mind under unendurable and fearful conditions. For thirty-seven days, she was in the dungeon, which was followed by inhuman torture. Just imagine a young girl of thirteen years enduring all this on her own! She still did not budge! The Emperor's men were then ordered to drown her, but that did not work either! In desperation, the Emperor, feeling defeated and also afraid that her miracles would convince the masses of the virtues of Christianity, condemned her to death and she was beheaded in Rome.

HER TOMB IS DISCOVERED

During the 18th century, Europe faced revolution, war, famine, atheism and persecution. So, Christians were forced to perform the sacred rites of their religion in the underground caverns (crypts) that were on every side of Rome. These caverns were constructed at great expense by wealthy Christian families as places of burial. During three consecutive centuries, the catacombs, as they are called, were also places where the faithful had their altars, and where they met to pray together. Until the raids by the Goths and Lombards, during which caskets were plundered and often completely destroyed, the catacombs were used to bury saints and martyrs. It must be noted that treasures were usually buried with the bodies of eminent people of that time. However, when peace returned, it was decided that the relics of popes and martyrs, which were still in the catacombs, would be removed to the safety of churches in Rome. This endeavour started at the beginning of the 8th century, right up to the time of Pope St. Paschal, when the catacombs were finally emptied.

Or so, everyone thought.

Time passed, memories faded, the whereabouts of the catacombs were completely forgotten...until, quite by accident, they were discovered by a labourer on 24 May 1802. An excited group of priests, physicians and excavators went to the catacomb of St. Priscilla to open the tomb of the little martyr. Her relics were then carried to Rome for safekeeping and then taken from there to Mugnano. A church was built for her in Mugnano, near Naples.

HOW SHE BECAME A SAINT

Since the discovery of her tomb in Rome in 1802, St. Philomena, martyred at just thirteen years of age, soon came to be recognized for her astonishing powers, mostly in curing incurable diseases. She is also known as the saint who 'brings joy to the sorrowful'.

MASS TODAY

Mass is performed daily in Kannada, Tamil and English at St. Philomena's Church. Behind a table is an exquisite marble altar on which the statue of St. Philomena is placed. There is also an idol of Christ lying down. Above the altar there are lovely stained glass windows from France showing important occasions in Jesus Christ's life. The towers resemble those of a cathedral in Cologne in Germany and of St. Patrick's Cathedral in New York.

On 10 August 1835, Pauline, a woman of great influence, who had been suffering from a supposedly incurable heart ailment, was suddenly cured at the St. Philomena's shrine in Mugnano del Cardinale. She was sure it had been a miracle and asked Pope Gregory XVI to begin the research required to proclaim Philomena (or Filumena) as a martyr saint. Almost two years later, after a thorough examination, Pope Gregory XVI declared St. Philomena as Patroness of the Living Rosary on 13 January 1837. A special feast day in her honour was declared too, along with a special Mass.

This is the *only* instance of a proper office being granted in honour of a saint from the catacombs, of whom nothing was known except her name and the fact of her martyrdom!

CUT TO JUNE 2019

The renovation of St. Philomena's Church is almost complete except for its exterior portions. The bishop blessed the renovated church on 17 June and regular Mass will now be held inside the church after a gap of one year. All these days, the Mass was being held outside the Church.

The entire church is built in the neo-gothic style and is one of the largest cathedrals in South Asia. It is no longer just a religious place but has also become a major tourist attraction in Mysuru. There is an orphanage on the premises of the church that is run by the church. An annual feast is held on 11 August each year.

THE MAN BEHIND IT ALL

Bernard Trichinopoly Thumboo Chetty, known as T. Thumboo Chetty, entered the Mysore Civil Service in 1904 as an assistant commissioner. In 1914, when Chetty joined the palace administration, his efficiency impressed Maharaja Krishna Raja Wadiyar who appointed him as the assistant secretary in his personal staff in November 1914.

GOOD WORK IN HER NAME

Holy women who devote themselves to good work in the name of the Saint are known as the Monacelle, or Little Sisters of St. Philomena. The order of the Little Sisters of St. Philomena was founded by Don Francesco in honour of the Saint.

By 1922, T. Thumboo Chetty was the Huzur secretary to Maharaja Krishna Raja Wadiyar, who held Chetty in very high esteem and therefore, entrusted him with the entire responsibility of educating and training Sri Jayachamarajendra Wadiyar as the future ruler of Mysore. Chetty later became the private secretary to Maharaja Jayachamarajendra Wadiyar from 1942 to 1949, who, at his birthday durbar in 1942, bestowed upon Chetty one of the highest titles—Amatya Siromani.

ALL FOR A DAUGHTER...

One of T. Thumboo Chetty's daughters was named Philomena by Reverend Father Jean-Bapiste Servanton, when she was baptized at St. Francis Xavier's Church, Bengaluru. Even though Chetty knew that his daughter had been named after the famous saint, he did not know much about her or her miracles.

In fact, it was one of his brothers, a devout believer and follower of St. Philomena, who urged Chetty many years later, to try and acquire a relic of his favourite saint from Italy, by using his position. He told him that the relics of St. Philomena were preserved not far from Mugnano. So, in 1926, Chetty wrote to the Right Reverend Monsignor Peter Pisani, who had been the Delegate Apostolic of India for some years and was then living in Rome. He requested him to try and send him a relic of St. Philomena. He waited for quite a while, but did not receive any reply. After a few months, Chetty went on a tour with the Maharaja to north India. While returning after visiting several places in the Himalayas, when they had made a stop in Benares, Chetty was surprised to receive a parcel from Rome. This packet had been redirected from place to place, following the royal party. It contained a relic of the Saint, together with a certificate of the Bishop Augustine Zampini of Rome, testifying the genuineness of it and giving permission for the relic to be on public display so that all devotees could pray to it. Chetty presented the relic to Reverend Father J. Cochet who was then in charge of St. Joseph's Church, Mysore. And, on 10 October 1927, the birthday of Chetty's little daughter, the bishop of Mysore blessed the statue and the relic, and for the first time, let the public also witness them both.

T. Thumboo Chetty retired in 1949 after serving the Mysore Princely State for over forty-five years. He remained totally devoted to St. Philomena all his life. If it hadn't been for his audacious request, there was no way a precious relic from Italy would ever have been worshipped in a cathedral in Mysuru, was there?

Miracles do happen, they say! What do you think?

10
The Gate with a Bloody History

Khooni Darwaza

You could not find a more innocent-looking structure if you tried. Nondescript, almost. Most who do not know better, barely give it a cursory glance when they happen to spot it. But get closer if you dare and have a real good look. Khooni Darwaza literally means 'The Bloody Gate'. It is a gate of the sixth city of Delhi. Some of the gates in the other cities are the Delhi Gate, the Kashmiri Gate and the Ajmeri Gate. These three are well-known landmarks.

Khooni Darwaza is one of the thirteen surviving gates in a good condition in Delhi. It was constructed by Sher Shah Suri. If only walls could talk!

Khooni Darwaza, also spelt Khuni Darwaza, is situated on the Bahadur Shah Zafar road, opposite Feroz Shah Kotla and was previously known as Kabuli Darwaza due to the fact that the road from this gate led to Kabul. If you ever visit this place, you will hear stories that in the monsoon, one can see blood dripping from the ceiling of this gate! Eeks! Just imagine the sight! However, a scientific explanation is that it is actually the rust from the joints of the gate that drips when it comes in contact with water, having a reddish colour that can be mistaken for blood!

GATES, GATES AND MORE GATES!

Delhi, for some odd reason, seems to be a city of gates. In 1611, European merchant William Finch had described Delhi as the city of seven castles (forts) and fifty-two gates.

Just imagine that! How would any new visitor figure out which gate to enter from? And of course, they all had names. More gates were built after that period during the Mughal rule and the British rule.

MUGHAL ARCHITECTURE

Mughal architecture is the type of Indo-Islamic architecture developed by the Mughals in the 16th, 17th and 18th centuries; a mixture of Islamic, Persian, Turkish and Indian architecture. Mughal buildings have a uniform pattern of structure, including large domes, minarets at the corners, massive halls, large gateways and delicate ornamentation. Shah Jahan, who constructed the breathtakingly beautiful Taj Mahal in Agra, and the Jama Masjid and the Red Fort in Delhi, got this kind of architecture noticed all over the world.

How many kings and queens has Delhi been ruled by? Belonging to so many different cultures, many of them left their mark on this city in one form or another. The historical monuments found all around Delhi are a testimony to these rulers' almost-obsessive yen to leave behind something permanent, for posterity.

This gate we are referring to was originally called

Lal Darwaza, or Red Gate. A nice innocent name, one would think. It was just one of the many, many gates built by the Pashtun Sher Shah Suri round his city Shergarh, while he ruled Delhi from 1540-45. But over the years, for some reason or the other, this gate ended up being the venue for very cruel and gory murders. So, it is no surprise that, somewhere along the way, the name got changed to Khooni Darwaza! The 'bloody trail' started with Jahangir's actions.

JAHANGIR'S REVENGE

Jahangir so wanted the throne after his father Emperor Akbar's death that he was ready to do anything for it—even punish anyone who even *thought* differently on this subject! One such strong and capable person who felt that Khusrau, Akbar's eldest son, should be the next emperor instead of Jahangir, was Abdul Rahim Khan-i-Khana. Rahim made the mistake of making his thoughts public. This led to a dual tragedy in his life.

Let's go back in time a little. Rahim was the son of Bairam Khan, who had helped Akbar and acted as his regent after Akbar's father, Emperor Humayun's death. Akbar had named Rahim as one of his Navratnas, or respected figures in his court. Jahangir developed a certain dislike towards him, which intensified when Rahim supported Khusrau's claim to the throne after Akbar's death. Rahim was also instrumental in getting the support of Raja Man Singh and Mirza Aziz for Khusrau. However, Jahangir still became the emperor of India and in order to get back at Rahim, he had both his sons executed at Khooni Darwaza. Their bodies were left hanging there for days to make an example out of them!

AURANGZEB'S ALL-CONSUMING AMBITION

The hunger and greed for the Mughal throne did not end there. There was yet another bitter struggle between brothers that took place when Dara Shikoh was declared the heir to the Mughal throne by Emperor Shah Jahan himself, which made things worse for him. He was the eldest and the most-favoured son of Shah Jahan. This favouritism gave rise to animosity among the other three brothers. Dara was favoured not just by his father but also by his older sister, Princess Jahanara Begum. He was not really a military man though; he was more inclined towards philosophy and the arts. He was liberal and unorthodox, quite a contrast to Aurangzeb who was very orthodox. On 10 September 1642, Shikoh was confirmed as the heir to his father's throne. His father conferred many titles on him—Padshahzada-i-Buzurg Martaba (Prince of High Rank) and Shahzada-e-Buland Iqbal (Prince of High Fortune). Shah Jahan also appointed his favourite son as the governor, first of Allahabad and then of Gujarat. Matters were alright, at least on the surface, until his father's health began to decline. He was appointed governor of Multan and Kabul on 16 August 1652, and was raised to the title of Shah-e-Buland Iqbal

(King of High Fortune) on 15 February 1655 by his doting father. But on 6 September 1657, the worsening of the health of Emperor Shah Jahan triggered a desperate struggle for power among the four Mughal princes, though only Dara Shikoh and Aurangzeb stood a chance of being victorious. At that point, all four of Shah Jahan's sons were governors of different parts of his kingdom. However, it was Prince Shah Shuja who made the first move, declaring himself as the Mughal emperor in Bengal and marching towards Agra, while Aurangzeb had Prince Murad on his side.

The unending support of his father and sister did not help Dara Shikoh much. Yes, he did defeat Shah Shuja in the battle of Bahadurpur on 14 February 1658, but Aurangzeb and Murad routed him in the Battle of Samugarhon just about three months later. Wasting no time, Aurangzeb took over the Agra Fort and imprisoned his father. Now that he was in full control of his father's kingdom, he did not need Murad's support anymore. So he imprisoned Murad in the Gwalior Fort! And as if that was not enough, the brother who had helped him get to power was executed on 4 December 1661 on a trumped-up charge of the murder of the diwan of Gujarat.

After the loss at the Battle of Samugarhon, Shikoh's luck did not change. He fled to Delhi. Then he gathered his army again for the final battle of his life—the battle of Deoraj on 11 March 1659. He lost. He fled. He then asked Malik Jiwan (Junaid Khan Barozai), an Aghan chieftain, for protection, probably assuming that since he had saved

Jiwan from being trampled to death by elephants on Shah Jahan's orders, this would be a good time for Jiwan to repay his debt. But no, that was not to be. Malik Jiwan betrayed him and handed him over to Aurangzeb! Aurangzeb then had his brother sit atop a dirty elephant and paraded through Delhi, but he had not bargained for the support that Shikoh had of the people. They berated Aurangzeb and Malik Jiwan for how they humiliated Shikoh. Aurangzeb realized that he could not afford to keep his brother alive and let the sympathy of the people grow for their prince and risk a revolt. So the wicked, wily Aurangzeb accused him of considering all religions equal and comparing Allah to other gods of the Hindu people. The trial happened in front of qazis and mullahs, which was nothing but a mockery of justice. Dara was convicted.

The charge of his assassination was given to slave Nazir. Nazir and four other assassins entered the prison in which Dara was kept with his son. One of them pulled his son Sipihr Shikoh away from him and Nazir beheaded him while his young son watched. The decapitated head was placed on a plate and shown to Aurangzeb as proof that it was indeed his brother Dara Shikoh who had been decapitated. Legend has it that Aurangzeb ordered that the head be put in a box and presented to his ailing father! Can you imagine the horror and sorrow Shah Jahan must have gone through? Shikoh's head was hung at the by-now-infamous Khooni Darwaza for days, as a warning to anyone who was against Emperor Aurangzeb!

AKBAR'S NAVRATNAS (NINE GEMS)

Akbar had appointed nine of his advisors, who helped him open his way of thinking to a new level of tolerance. They were: Birbal, Tansen, Abu'l Fazal, Faizi, Man Singh, Todar Mal, Mullah Do-Piyaza, Aziao-Din and Abdul Rahim Khan-i-Khana.

Birbal was the main commander of Akbar's army, but his witty responses in the court of Akbar made him more famous as a jester. Tansen was a musician in Akbar's court. Abu'l Fazal was the author of Akbarnama and Ain-i-Akbari. Abu'l Fazal's brother Faizi, whose real name was Shaikh Abu al-Faiz ibn Mubarak, was a poet with the status of Malik-ush-Shu'ara (Poet Laureate). Man Singh was the king of Amber, a general in Akbar's army and the grandson of Akbar's father-in-law Bharmal. Todar Mal was the finance minister of the Mughal Empire during Akbar's reign. Mullah Do-Piyaza was an advisor to Akbar, though historians claim that he is a fictional character, having never been mentioned in the historical texts of Akbar's time. Aziao-Din was a sufi mystic and an advisor to Akbar on religious matters. And Abdul Rahim Khan-i-Khana was a poet and the son of Bairam Khan, Akbar's trusted guardian and mentor.

HODSON'S FOLLY

Many decades later, Bahadur Shah Zafar, the last Mughal emperor, was accepted as the emperor of India by the rebels of the Indian Rebellion of 1857, also known as the First War of Independence. He named his eldest surviving son, Mirza Mughal, as the commander-in-chief. However, the inexperience and indiscipline of the Indian soldiers led to their defeat. British forces suppressed the rebellion. Major William Hodson obtained the surrender of the emperor, and the next day asked for an unconditional surrender from the three princes at Humayun's Tomb. The princes, who were probably suspicious, had refused to surrender, demanding guarantees of safety. On the following day, with about 100 horsemen, Hodson returned to insist on an unconditional surrender from the princes. A huge crowd gathered in support of the princes. Hodson did not want a skirmish, so he ordered the crowd to disarm themselves. They all followed his order. While ninety of his men collected the arms from the crowd, Hodson sent ten of his men with the princes to Delhi on a bullock cart along with sixteen members of the royal family.

As they approached the city gate, a crowd of people again started to gather around them, and Hodson ordered the three princes of the Mughal dynasty—Bahadur Shah Zafar's sons Mirza Mughal and Mirza Khizr Sultan and grandson Mirza Abu Bakht—to get off the cart and to strip off their top garments. He then took a carbine from one of his troopers and shot them dead at point-blank range, but not before stripping them of their signet rings, turquoise arm bands and bejewelled swords. Their bodies were ordered to be displayed in front of a kotwali, or police station, near Chandni Chowk, and left there to be seen by all. This tragedy occurred on 22 September 1857. Hodson's actions were controversial even at the time. Bahadur Shah II was put on trial. However, since Hodson had previously guaranteed his life, he was exiled to Rangoon (now called Yangon), in Burma (or Myanmar), where he died in November 1862 at the age of eighty-seven.

THE STRUCTURE

Khooni Darwaza is a double-storied structure with an archway. It was built largely with grey stone but red stones were also used in the frames of its windows. You will really have to look for it on Mathura Road near Maulana Azad Medical College. Khooni Darwaza is today a protected monument under the Archaeological Survey of India. The gate is 15.5-metres (50.9-feet) high and built with Delhi quartzite stone. Three staircases lead to different levels of the gate, a perfectly innocent-looking structure that you are more than likely to miss while going down that road.

CONCLUSION

With such a gruesome history, it is no wonder that the gate is believed to be haunted by the ghosts of the many people who died here under such tragic circumstances! Some people even claim to have seen blood on the walls of the structure during daytime! Stories and rumours will keep on growing, with imagination running riot.

11
The Drowning Church
Shettihalli Rosary Church

To get the full benefit of the magnificence of this church, one would have to make two trips during the year. No point, otherwise. The awe-inspiring spires and the ability to walk through the church in the winter and summer months (December to May) is an altogether different experience to that when the church is almost completely submerged during the pelting monsoon (July to October) that is typical of this region. Submerged, did we say? Yes! Not totally, but submerged for sure! Surreal is the only word that fits these experiences.

THE FRENCH CONNECTION

It is said that the Shettihalli Rosary Church was built by French missionaries in the 1860s. It is the finest example of gothic architecture and used to be a fully functioning church, reportedly built with mortar and bricks and a mixture of jaggery and eggs! This gothic-style church was constructed on the picturesque banks of Hemavathi River in Hassan and served the wealthy British living around, as a religious centre of worship. It is also said that there was a village that surrounded the church. However, after the Gorur-Hemavathi dam/reservoir was planned in 1960, the Shettihali Rosary Church was abandoned.

So, have any of you seen or heard of a church that drowns every monsoon and emerges during the summers? Well, this is it! It has stood the test of time, in spite of being under water for so many months every single year for almost forty years! Shettihalli is a small village situated on the banks of the Gorur-Hemavathi reservoir, which is about 25 kilometres from Hassan in Karnataka. The drowning church is located 22 kilometres from the Shettihalli village itself.

HEMAVATHI RIVER

The 245-kilometre-long Hemavathi River starts in the Western Ghats at an elevation of about 1,219 metres near Ballalarayana Durga in Chikmagalur District, Karnataka. It flows through Tumkur, Hassan District, where it is joined by its chief tributary, the Yagachi River, and then into Mandya District before joining the Kaveri River near Krishnarajasagara.

Let us go back in time a bit. The government had decided to build the Gorur-Hemavathi dam so that the flowing river could become more useful. In its heyday, prior to the construction of the reservoir at Gorur, Shettihalli used to be a very rich agricultural hub that was known for its sunflower fields. However, after the Gorur reservoir was constructed so that the water of the Hemavathi River could be put to better use, the subsequent collateral damage during the process led to the submersion of around twenty-eight villages around the river. We all know that dams and reservoirs require relocation of large human populations if the dams are constructed close to residential areas. All the inhabitants of these villages were therefore relocated to nearby villages. The church was also part of the collateral damage and hence was abandoned forever in 1960.

The sight of the eerily intact structure of the Rosary Church is disconcerting at first sight. What got damaged the most over all these years was the roof of the church. The present roofless structure is located in a barren field, and is a relatively unexplored location, off the beaten tourist path. The entire roof has caved in, while part of the altar and the central nave still stand, but there are no artistic stained glass windows, pews for worshippers to kneel on or even windows or doors left in the church.

Not many travel there, though it is visited by research scholars and architecture students. Today, the church is home to some birds in the non-monsoon months. What a pity! Can you imagine the weddings that must have taken place within the walls of the once-magnificent church? The Christmas Mass, the devoted gathering, the christenings of babies...

As the summer gives way to the monsoon, the waters of the Hemavathi rise. Slowly, but surely, part by part, the Shettihalli Church drowns in it, nearly submerged except for its lonely topmost spire sticking out of the water like a helpless beacon when the reservoir is near to its brim.

And, when the waters recede, the Shettihalli Church ruins strike a stark contrast to the vividly coloured landscape around it, emerging in all its glory. That is Shettihalli's only claim to limited fame, a deserted spot where people sometimes come to see the half-submerged church during monsoons and a completely visible church when the water recedes. Even locals admit that the gothic-inspired structure does give the Rosary Church haunted vibes.

THE DAM IN QUESTION

If you want to watch the dam in action, go when the local paper announces that water is to be let out of the dam, but also prepare for it to be very crowded then. On other days, the location is very serene and makes for a very good picnic spot. The Gorur dam is constructed across the Hemavathy River, a tributary of the Kaveri River. The dam is about 20 kilometres from Hassan. Completed in 1979, with a length of 4,692 metres and a height of 58.5 metres, it has six large radial spillway gates. When the gates of the reservoir are opened, the water gushes down in cascades. The best time to visit the dam is during the months of August to November, when there is more water in the dam. Children from schools nearby are regularly brought to view the dam. Funnily enough, most tourists make the effort to go and admire the water gushing out of the open gates of the dam, while not even knowing of the existence of the Rosary Church on the other side within the reservoir itself.

WHAT ELSE?

Of late, the area around the church is used for shooting regional movies and serials. Haunted films, we guess! For those who are keen on photography, this place makes a perfect subject. When the dark sky shows through the Shettihalli Church, with the Hemavathi River in the background, it creates the most amazing panoramic view. Bird lovers and nature enthusiasts make the effort to visit and admire the breathtaking surroundings, scenic landscapes, valleys, green fields, trees, cool waterbodies and the summer breeze, soaking in the peace. A serendipitous trip to the church is truly magical, like looking for a lost city; in this case, an almost-lost church. There will be birds, cattle and reptiles for company. When the water level is low, coracles (small round boats) are sometimes used to go inside the church.

While there are few records that mention that the said church was constructed in 1860, nobody really has a clue. Local villagers say it was built some 160 years back. Anyway, once a year, around April, when the church is not underwater, local people conduct prayers with lamps. When all is said and done, there is something eerie *and* serene about the spot. Paranormal probably?

12

The Temple with Musical Pillars

Vittala Temple

*S*a, Re, Ga, Ma pillars? Yes! That is what the famous musical pillars in the Vittala Temple in Hampi are called. This temple is an ancient structure, well-known for its architecture and unmatched craftsmanship. The monument is easily one of the largest and most famous structures in the group of monuments in Hampi. Located in the northeastern part of Hampi near the banks of the Tungabhadra River, it is difficult not to be affected by the stunning beauty and workmanship that is showcased on these stones.

VITTALA BAZAAR

This is one of the many ancient bazaars in Hampi. As the name indicates, Vittala Bazaar is attached to the iconic Vittala Temple, at the west end. This street is still intact and functional. The bazaar is in a general east-west orientation, parallel to the Tungabhadra River nearby. One way to reach Vittala Bazaar (and Vittala Temple) is by a short trek along the riverside from the Hampi Bazaar end.

HAMPI

This area has many other beautiful stone structures too, like the stone chariot, the Goddess's shrine in the northwest, the 100-pillared hall in the southwest, the Kalyana Mantapa (the ceremonial marriage hall) in the southeast and the pillared cloisters all around the enclosure wall. But the temple remains the major draw amongst tourists who come from across the globe to glimpse the once-glorious Vijayanagara capital, which lies in ruins now. Schools nearby also organize cycle rides to this monumental outdoor museum.

Just imagine what it must have been like to be living there, so many years ago. The monuments take you back to the early 15th century, when the structure was built during the rule of Deva Raya II (1422–1446), who was one of the more famous rulers of the Vijayanagara Empire, and sensitive to the arts and crafts. Krishnadevaraya (1509–1529), the most famous ruler of the Vijayanagara kingdom, expanded the temple during his reign.

Hampi falls within the state of Karnataka, about 350 kilometres from Bengaluru. It is an absolute delight for any student or lover of history, archaeology, architecture or religion. Spread over 25 square kilometres, one would probably need a whole week to do proper justice to its many temples, palaces and other awe-inspiring stone monuments. On top of that, you have giant boulders strewn all over the terrain, as well as a river that bisects the area...

No wonder it is on the list of UNESCO's World Heritage Sites.

One of the best ways to enter the Hampi grounds is from the eastern entrance tower. Very soon you will come upon the famous stone chariot, which shows up on practically any poster or book cover of these world-famous ruins. One look at that image and one immediately knows that Hampi is being referred to. The chariot is actually a temple, albeit a very unusual one. The stone chariot temple was dedicated to the Eagle God, Garuda, who is the vahana (vehicle) of Lord Vishnu. So, it is indeed befitting that this temple faces the main temple. If you lie down and peep under the chariot, you will be rewarded with the sight of a relatively well-preserved painting, typical of those times when art, music and dance flourished in the Vijayanagara kingdom. Being underneath the chariot, the painting was protected better than the rest of the sculptures of the Vittala Temple, which are said to have been covered with similar paintings. Can you imagine that these large wheels of the chariot would be turned by visitors a long time ago?

VITTALA TEMPLE

This temple, also known as the Shri Vijaya Vittala Temple, is proof of the immense creativity and architectural expertise possessed by the sculptors and artisans of the Vijayanagara Empire. The temple is built in the Dravidian style of architecture. One can imagine the sight of so many skilled sculptors chiselling away at massive chunks of stone, slowly turning them into the masterpieces that we see today.

The temple stands in a large rectangular enclosure of 164 metres by 94.5 metres. Aim to reach the main Mahamantapa (the Great Hall) as soon as possible. After all, for many it is the highlight of the visit. The hall, it is said, had been partially damaged by Mughal conquerors in 1565. Obviously meant for the mighty and important, the Mahamantapa is literally on a higher plane—elevated and special.

Four open halls fall within the Mahamantapa. While the southern, northern and eastern halls are quite intact, the main hall has caved in a bit. The central western hall has collapsed. The main highlight of the Mahamantapa is its richly carved giant monolithic pillars. The outermost of the pillars are called the musical pillars.

The musician's hall, which is the eastern hall, has elaborate sculptures of musicians and dancers on its walls.

For some unknown and slightly bewildering reason, the southern hall is covered with sculptures of mythical creatures called Yalis—part lion, part elephant and part horse—somewhat incongruent to the rest of the art around.

Legend has it that this temple, which is dedicated to Vittala, an incarnation of Lord Vishnu, was originally built to serve as a home for Lord Vishnu in this particular incarnation. However, it is said that when it was completed, he found it much too grand for him and chose to return to his simple home in Pandharpur.

MUSICAL PILLARS

The large Ranga Mantapa, with its famous fifty-six musical pillars, emits musical notes when the pillars are gently tapped with one's thumb. Sa, Re, Ga, Ma are four of the seven musical notes as per Indian classical music, the rest being Pa, Da, Ni. Each pillar is 3.6-metres high and made of solid granite. These huge pillars also provide vital support to the roof of the mantapa.

The main pillars are designed as musical instruments and every main pillar has seven minor pillars that emit musical sounds. Every note coming out of these pillars varies in its sound quality and also changes as per the percussion, string or wind instrument being played. Now let us think aloud: How do these pillars of the same material create different sounds? Were holes created in the granite? If so, that would explain the various sounds that the pillars produce. The British tried to figure this mystery out by cutting one of the larger pillars and one of the smaller ones too, to get to the bottom of this mystery. But there was no revelation, because all the pillars were the same—solid rock!

If the height, weight or diametre had been altered, the chances of the pillars making different sounds would be high. But no, no, no. All the columns are of the same height, weight and diametre. And still they produce these musical notes! No credible explanation! However, tapping the musical pillars has now been prohibited, as tapping over the years has caused some damage to the musical pillars.

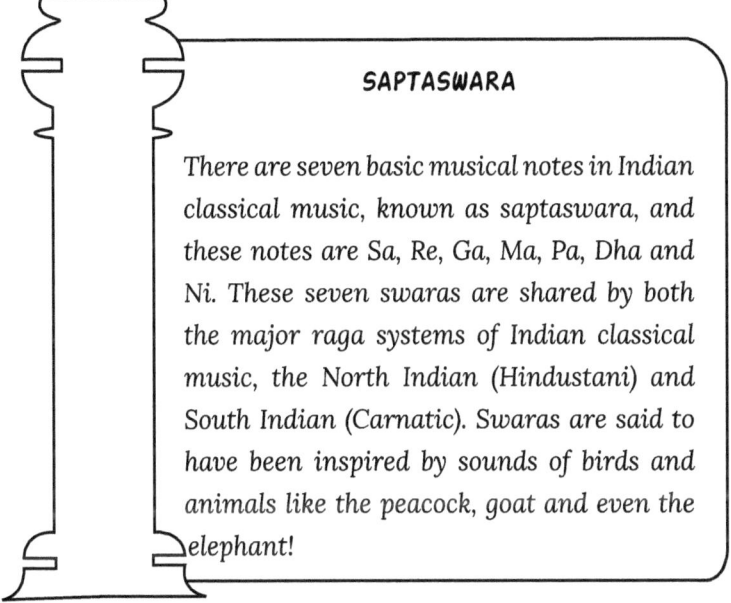

SAPTASWARA

There are seven basic musical notes in Indian classical music, known as saptaswara, and these notes are Sa, Re, Ga, Ma, Pa, Dha and Ni. These seven swaras are shared by both the major raga systems of Indian classical music, the North Indian (Hindustani) and South Indian (Carnatic). Swaras are said to have been inspired by sounds of birds and animals like the peacock, goat and even the elephant!

FINALLY, RESEARCH!

Scientists from the Indira Gandhi Centre for Atomic Research in Kalpakkam, Tamil Nadu, conducted the first scientific investigation on the acoustic properties of the musical columns in the pillars around 2006-07. The study was concentrated on the eleven most popular pillars. Non-destructive techniques such as low-frequency ultrasonic testing and in-situ metallography were used. The in-situ metallography revealed that the microstructure of the pillars were similar to a typical granite microstructure. The low-frequency ultrasonic and impact echo testing showed that all the musical columns are solid shafts. Most of the musical instruments that the sounds from the pillars correlated to were percussion instruments like the Kerala mridangam, tabla, ghatam and damaru. The other musical sounds were that of the veena, jaltarang, shankha, ghanta, panchtala and saptaswara. So, so fascinating, isn't it?

12½
The Hide-and-Seek Beach
Chandipur Beach

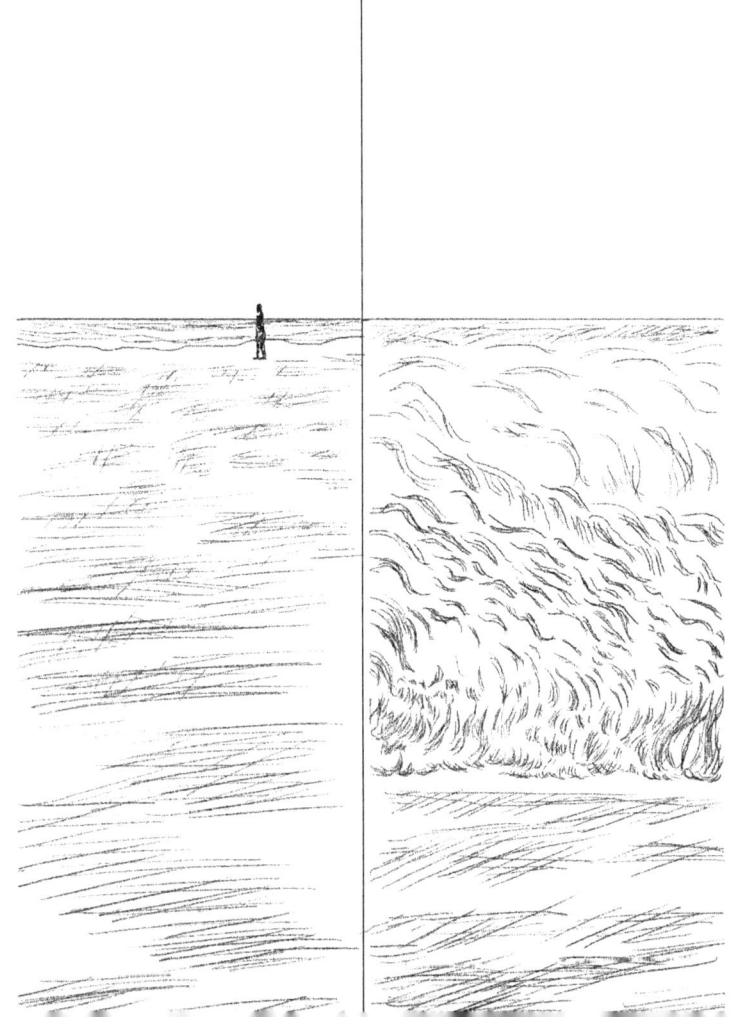

Think of magic, of stage shows, of illusionists and conjurors. Now, think of the great magicians of the world. What names pop up in your mind? David Copperfield? Criss Angel? P.C. Sorcar? Or Gogia Pasha? What if we told you that the greatest magician of them all is Nature? Yes, that's true! The velvety texture of a flower, lush green forests, the cool experience of a flowing stream, the splendid climate of different places, the soothing showers of monsoon are all different parts of Nature's great magical act. And one such sleight of hand performed by Nature is in the form of a sea that vanishes right in front of your eyes, only to reappear hours later! Believe it or not, this beach in India is not a constantly existing feature on the map; at least it doesn't look the same every time! Surprised? Let us take you to Chandipur in Odisha to show you a beach that disappears in thin air! No kidding!

NOW YOU SEE IT, NOW YOU DON'T

Do you like to play hide-and-seek? The Chandipur Beach, some 200 kilometres from the capital city of Bhubaneswar, in Odisha, loves this game too! One of the wonders of nature, the waters of this magical sea vanish right before your eyes and come back rhythmically at regular intervals, as if playing hide-and-seek. This hide-and-seek game of the sea occurs twice a day. The sea disappears about— hold your breath!—5 to 6 kilometres during the low tides, replacing the area with sand dunes, and you can even walk on the waterbed that is left behind—without being washed away! (Doesn't this sound like a water trick that magicians perform so very often? See, didn't we tell you that Nature's the greatest magician and all that!) You can even play a game of football or enjoy a jeep ride on the seabed. During the high tides, the waters of the sea come back again. On most other beaches in the world, the waves come and go, dashing off the shore, but in Chandipur, the waves are like a musical fountain, soothing to the eyes and ears.

INTEGRATED RESEARCH RANGE

Another interesting fact about Chandipur is that it is home to the Defence Research and Development Organization (DRDO) Integrated Research Range, where ballistic missiles are test-fired. The Akash, Shaurya, Agni and Prithvi ballistic missiles have been launched from here. A scenic beach and missile launch site make for quite a unique combination, don't you think? Could there be a strange, inexplicable connection between the disappearing beach and the test range? Aha! Just think about it.

WOW! BUT HOW?

A strange phenomenon that is rarely seen in any other part of the world, experts say that this receding of the sea during ebb, and filling up the expanse again during flow, happens because of the large difference in the low and high tides. This phenomenon happens every single day at no fixed time. Everything depends on the moon's cycle. While the locals know when to expect the high and low tides, tourists are warned to stay clear of the beach during full moon and new moon days, for on those days the waves of the sea here hit unusual highs. Since the level of the sea depends on various factors like the earth's rotation and the forces exerted by the sun and the moon, isn't it strange that these factors result in such an unusual difference in sea levels only at this particular beach? Which is why the Chandipur Beach is globally known as the 'vanishing sea' beach.

SHADE CARD

Due to the difference in water levels across the vast Chandipur seabed, you can witness shades of the colour blue in neatly stacked parallel sections—making it look like a huge canvas of a divine painter who was obsessed with the colour blue!

Strange and Mysterious Places the World Forgot

A MELTING POT OF DIFFERENT SPECIES

Another remarkable feature of the Chandipur Beach is that because of the unique slope of the seabed here, small waves form in the middle very unusually, shifting later. Due to its special shape and contour, this place supports a unique range of biodiversity. One can find the ruby-coloured rare Horseshoe crab here, which are often known as 'living fossils' (because the fossils of these crabs' ancestors date back to 450 million years ago, which is 200 million years before dinosaurs existed!). The beach also has an abundance of seashells, driftwood and king crabs. The washed-away seabed leaves a variety of seashells in different shapes and sizes. Also, you can spot many birds looking for food, such as small sea creatures like fishes and crabs, on the exposed seabed. When the water reappears, it brings along with it crabs scurrying across the sand, which otherwise live further away from the beach. Tortoises, small starfish or other sea creatures can also be found here. The beach is framed by Casuarina trees.

A MYSTERY YOU CAN VISIT

Humans have visited nearly every place on earth and even beyond. They've gone to the bottom of the ocean and they've walked on the moon. Yet there are so many mysterious places that fascinate us. Their stories feed our imagination and their mysteries inspire us to learn more about our amazing world. Chandipur Beach is one such place. A missing person is one thing—but a disappearing beach? Sounds like a great mystery story. But it's no fiction. It's real—as real as you can see; it is a place that you can visit. It is a miracle of nature, a mystery that leaves us with a lot of questions.

Stop and think!

How does the moon affect the tides?

Are there other disappearing beaches in the world?

What are some of the other magical tricks that Nature plays on us?

What other places would you call 'wonders of nature'? A long-lost cave, a mighty waterfall, an island arc, or a great, big chasm?

If these are questions that spark your curiosity, there's a young investigator inside you who's waiting to get on the job. You can try and figure out the answers for yourself. Do your own research by digging around online (safely, of course!), fiddling about in your school or public library, or asking your teacher or other adults around you for help. Don't be shy—asking questions is the best way to learn! After you're done with your research, try and come up with your own list of mysterious places that you didn't even know existed. Maybe, just maybe, someday you would want to visit these places to investigate them in person and uncover the mysteries that lurk about them! Sounds like a fun thing to do, doesn't it?

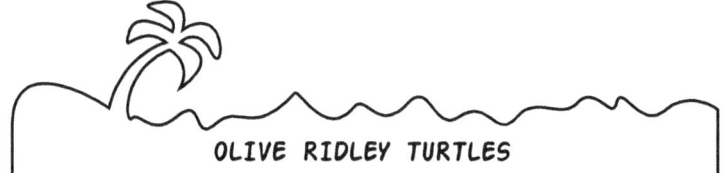

OLIVE RIDLEY TURTLES

Incidentally, much before he became the president of India, Dr A.P.J. Abdul Kalam had helped in a mission that was crucial to the survival of the endangered Olive Ridley turtles. As the then chief of DRDO, when his attention was drawn to the fact that the Olive Ridley turtles, which have their largest rookery in the world on the Gahirmatha beach in Odisha, were being distracted by the bright lights on the Wheeler Island missile testing facility nearby, he ensured that the lights were masked during the nesting season. The island was later renamed Abdul Kalam Island.

MY LIST OF MYSTERIOUS PLACES

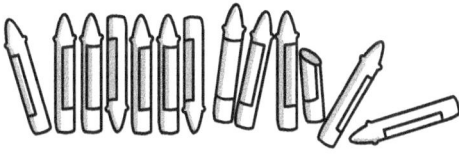

_____

_____

Acknowledgements

It takes a village to write a book. It really does. A big and wonderful village. We owe many grateful thanks to each one of the immensely helpful people who joined us in our journey of turning the germ of an idea into this full-fledged book.

Combing a country as big as a continent to arrive at just 'twelve-and-a-half' places wasn't the easiest of tasks and we'd like to thank the team at Rupa Publications for all the thoughtful suggestions. We would also like to thank our editors for their promptness, gentle but persistent feedback and editorial finesse.

We thank our families for keeping things on track while we were on our armchair travels across the country…and for everything they have always done and continue to do.

And last, but not the least, we thank Mistunee Chowdhury for bringing the stories alive with her beautiful black-and-white illustrations.

www.ingramcontent.com/pod-product-compliance
Lightning Source LLC
Chambersburg PA
CBHW070546090426
42735CB00013B/3081